THE FOUR
VOICES OF MAN

THE FOUR
VOICES OF MAN

JEROME
HINES

LIMELIGHT EDITIONS
New York

First Limelight Edition November 1997

Library of Congress Cataloging-in-Publication Data

Hines, Jerome, 1921–
    The four voices of man / by Jerome Hines.
    p.   cm.
    ISBN 0-87910-099-0
    1. Singing. 2. Vocal registers. 3. Singing—Vocational guidance.
4. Opera—Vocational guidance.   I. Title.
    MT820.H655   1997
    783'.043—dc20

                       97-20989
                         CIP
                         MN

Book design and composition by Emdash, Inc.

A word of caution:

If you are *not* at an advanced level of training,
PLEASE KEEP THIS BOOK ON THE SHELF

until

**YOUR TEACHER RECOMMENDS THAT
YOU READ IT.***

*If, when you are ready, your teacher fails
to direct you to this book, get another teacher!

TABLE OF CONTENTS

ACKNOWLEDGEMENTS

My eternal gratitude to my beloved Lucia,
critic sans-souci and to whom I wholeheartedly dedicate this book.

Thanks to all the artists I interviewed in *Great Singers On Great Singing* and who gave me so much to think about. And thanks to the following who contributed so much to my career and understanding (listed chronologically):

Lucy McCullough, who discovered my voice and then selflessly pushed me out of the nest.

Gennaro M. Curci, who did such a fabulous job of teaching me and launching my career.

Lauritz Melchior, who proved to me that high is really low.

Rocco Pandiscio, who first taught me to sing as I speak: without taking a breath.

Robert Merrill, who influenced me to continue my studies under Samuel Margolis and advised me to use pure undistorted vowels and never give more than 90 percent of my voice.

Samuel Margolis, who gave me the vocal discipline that leads to longevity.

Val Rosing, who taught me to give the audience an experience, not a singing lesson.

Eleanor Steber, who showed me the true meaning of steel in the spine.

Jussi Bjoerling, who informed me that one's lips should not be used for making vowels.

Ezio Pinza, who demonstrated the importance of doing everything authoritatively.

Emil Cooper, who taught me the ideal singer/conductor relationship.

Kurt Baum, who advised me to use low support and sparing breath on high notes.

Ramon Vinay, who taught me to be serious on the stage.

Fausto Cleva, who taught me great respect and love for musical discipline.

Alberto Erede, who gave me a deeper understanding of Italian pronunciation and diction.

Dr. Arthur D'Alessandro, who led me to apply ultrasound to the larynx.

Dr. Leo P. Reckford, who showed me the distinction between falsetto and chest voice.

John Leslie, who inspired me to always come back fighting.

Arturo Toscanini, who demanded the impossible from us imperfect mortals.

Bruno Walter, who showed me that Mozart should be performed with heart.

Leonard Warren, who gave me a better understanding of the high voice.

Paul Hume, who showed me that great critics are also great men.

Jay Harrison, who made me realize that critics are just as human as the rest of us.

Dr. Robert Jones, who advised me on the physiology of breathing, and oversaw my chapter on Support/Appoggio.

Ruth Dobson, who first made me realize that I also had a woman's voice.

Joseph McClellan, who so rightly advocated loving your profession rather than its perks.

Frank Corsaro, who showed me that there is no substitute for genius.

Lulu I (our poodle), who gave me some really profitable ideas about acting.

Joaquim Romaguera, who supplied me with the term "shoehorn effect."

Joseph Shore, who gave me a better understanding of the male's high voice.

Eileen Strempel, who led me to use Echinacea to prevent the common cold.

Dodie Protero, who made me aware of "whistle tones."

Shelley Jameson, who confirmed my opinion about "whistle tones."

Reegan McKenzie, who gave me a better understanding of "whistle tones."

Mark Delavan, who modified Caruso's "square throat" to a "rhomboid."

Miguel Sanchez Moreno, who showed me how to support by low, lateral expansion.

And thanks to the occasional student who taught *me* something by doing what I couldn't.

So now you know who I studied with—EVERYBODY!

PREFACE

This book evolved out of the writing of *Great Singers on Great Singing* (Doubleday, 1982). I was initially tempted to call it "What My Teachers Never Taught Me," a title that was not intended as a put down for the teacher, but as a means of directing attention to a very real problem: many people have exaggerated expectations regarding the student/teacher relationship—and "many people" includes teachers, as well as students. I had three teachers, each of whom was of great help to me, but not one of them had all the answers. Some problems I had to resolve by myself.

I do not buy the Svengali approach to teaching in which the singer is just a piece of clay to be molded by the potter. Leave that to God! A student must actively take part in the creative process—with the teacher in charge, of course. But more about that later.

Although I will primarily discuss vocal technique, I will also spend considerable time on "career technique," since a great voice and vocal know-how do not a career make.

There are many critical factors that can frustrate an opera career and one must face them realistically—or else! Emotional instability, laziness, self-indulgence, dishonesty, unhealthy lifestyle are just some of the potentially fatal flaws that can afflict a singer, and need our serious attention. We must focus on self-discipline, motivation, how to deal with teachers, coaches, stage directors, conductors, managers, impresarios—and even critics. But our primary concern will still be proper use of the voice, without which you can forget all the rest.

Now, why am I writing this tome? Didn't I say it all when I authored *Great Singers on Great Singing*? Absolutely not! I literally said *nothing*, deliberately staying out of the way of my famous interviewees: it was to be their book, not mine. And why did I write it? I confess that I have a devious mind: how else could I get a free singing lesson from two score of the greatest scorers in operatic history?

Believe me, I learned more about vocal technique in the writing of that book than I had learned in all my previous years of study and I feel it has added many years to my vocal life. The effect has been so positive that I am anxious to share what I have gleaned from those interviews with anyone courageous enough to listen. So, YOU are the real reason why I am writing this book.

Now, I have no desire to become your role model: my lifestyle is too far-out to be emulated. To become an opera singer, would you spend six years in college majoring in organic chemistry, mathematics and physics—and without taking a single course in music?

Don't get the idea that I changed my mind along the way and switched to opera. I am not that deeply into Switchcraft. I decided to be an opera singer at the age of sixteen and immediately began private study with Gennaro M. Curci, the brother-in-law of the great coloratura soprano, Amelita Galli-Curci. By the time I was twenty, Maestro Curci had taught me twenty major operatic roles in their original languages and arranged for me to debut as a soloist with the San Francisco Opera.

Me, a role model? Let's face it, I was a freak—and still am! Where did I find the time for all this? It was easy, I was a social misfit in high school. What girl of sound mind would ever think of dating a six and a half foot scarecrow who weighed 150 pounds and was two years her junior? Time was all I had. Yet I've never regretted those lonely hours which taught me the joys of intro-spection and creativity. Now, as a performing artist, I know what to do with all that leisure time on tour: I write books, research papers, operas, songs, whatever pleases me.

That is the lifestyle I love, but I would never wish it on you. It is obviously not the definitive route to becoming an opera singer and I am not about to suggest that you, too, become a freak. However, you will soon discover that the life of a successful artist is not exactly a normal one. Prepare yourself for that so it will not come as a shock.

Did I waste all those years studying math and science? Hardly! It taught me to think logically—which, contrary to popular opinion, is not a hindrance to being an opera singer. So a bit of logic might come in handy in writing a treatise such as this. Don't knock it—profit!

I will now try to give you some sound advice on forging a career and, hopefully, it will present a balanced picture of Art wedded to Science. Prepare to unlimber both your left and right lobes—not of your lungs, but of your brain.

JEROME HINES

INTRODUCTION

So many books on vocal technique have flooded the marketplace that I hesitate to add to the confusion. There are even those who might brand me as guilty of having already contributed more than my share to this confusion by having authored *Great Singers on Great Singing*. In the midst of a flood of excellent reviews there did appear one or two discordant ones claiming the book to be so riddled with conflicting opinions that it would just add to the confusion already so prevalent.

I am always amazed when I encounter people whose mental myopia prevents them from discerning obvious truths. The soloists interviewed in *Great Singers on Great Singing* were all of such stature that they surely knew something about how to sing. If those tunnel-visioned critics would only recall the old adage, "There is more than one way to skin a cat," there might be some hope for them.

Were the great performers whom I interviewed for the book actually so deeply at odds with each other on vocal technique? And, if so, who was right and who was wrong? Many teachers and professionals claimed to find a common thread of logic woven throughout the interviews. And, as I first prepared the book, I also found many common threads. But in all honesty there did emerge some fundamental differences which cannot be ignored.

That is what led me to choose *The Four Voices of Man* as the title of this book. It will become evident that there are four distinctly different approaches to singing, all of which are viable and have enabled the world's greatest artists to have long, successful careers despite their differences in vocal technique.

I hope to approach the subject in a manner that will not upset reputable teachers—and they will not be upset if they are broad-minded enough to consider the premise that there might be other viable schools of singing different from their own. Naturally, there will always be those who have "the one and only technique" (Surely, wisdom shall die with them!) and they will emphatically disagree with this.

For example, when I visited Zinka Milanov in 1980, she firmly stated, "There is only one right way to sing—the way I do!"

Now, there is no disputing the fact that Zinka was one of the greatest singers of her generation, but she only sang repertoire with which she was comfortable. Unfortunately, we Americans are not allowed that luxury; we are forced to sing anything that comes along and we soon become painfully aware that Wagner (which I don't recall Zinka singing) is not sung with the same approach as is Mozart; nor is Mozart sung with the same approach as is Verdi. Shifting from one role to another will often require some sort of vocal adjustment.

One of my greatest challenges came in 1952 when, after singing the title role in Boito's *Mefistofele* in Buenos Aires, I flew directly to Munich where I sang the title role in *Don Giovanni*. No one will ever convince me that these two diverse roles can be sung with the same vocal approach.

In fact, Ezio Pinza, who was such a marvelous Don Giovanni, once heard me rehearsing Mefistofele in a Met dressing room and, bursting brusquely through the door, sternly warned me to never sing that role, saying it would destroy my voice. I was later told he had unsuccessfully attempted to sing Mefistofele at Teatro Colon, breaking on all his high notes, and then never sang it again. Obviously, he found that Mefistofele and Don Giovanni could not be played in the same ball park.

You cannot sing such diversified repertoire without shifting your technique to accommodate to the situation. I know, having extensively sung in operas by Bartók, Beethoven, Bellini, Boito, Britten, Catalani, Charpentier, Debussy, Delibes, Donizetti, Gounod, Handel, Hines, Mascagni, Massenet, Meyerbeer, Montemezzi, Moore, Moussorgsky, Mozart, Offenbach, Ponchielli, Poulenc,

Puccini, Strauss, Stravinski, Tchaikowski, Thomas, Verdi, Wagner—you name it—and have survived quite well for over half a century. If your teacher disagrees with me, ask how many years he/she has spent on the stage doing the varied repertoire I just listed.

As I said earlier, there are at least four diverse vocal techniques and we should not dogmatically call one right and the others wrong. Any technique that enables you to have a long, successful career is viable. And most likely your teacher has introduced you to at least one of the four.

If you have studied voice for several years, you have possibly arrived at a professional level in at least one of these four techniques. But when you leave the protected environment of the studio, you will immediately be subjected to such diverse opinions on how to use your voice that you can become confused to the point of saying, "Leave me alone, I don't want to hear any more of this."

The trouble is, your well meaning colleagues may assume you are singing incorrectly if you do not approach everything exactly as they do. That is hogwash! If your ideas differ from theirs it doesn't mean you are wrong, nor does it mean they are wrong! The real test is not your vocal ideology, but simple pragmatism. If something works well for you on the stage, what's wrong with that? Actually, you and your contradictive colleagues might all end up with successful careers, while doing things quite differently.

My advice is to trust (within reason) what you have been taught. You must be doing something right or you wouldn't have gotten as far as you have. So give your teacher a chance! Do not make it a habit to flit from studio to studio. Only if you are in serious vocal trouble and are convinced your teacher is to blame, should you switch.

After everything has gone reasonably well for a while and you feel adventurous, shop around and see if your colleagues are doing things you can't do. Then try to discover what is different about their technique. Experiment and gently incorporate some of their ideas into your singing—but with one basic axiom in mind: *Never acquire something new at the expense of losing something of the old.*

As you experiment with new things, constantly go back and be sure you can still do everything you were able to do before.

For example, one of the most common things I heard in my early days was, "You have terrible high notes because you sing much too heavily in the middle. You must thin out your low and middle voice."

Now that I have enjoyed having a good high voice for quite a few years—surprise, surprise—I can take the biggest, fattest sounds possible in my middle voice all the way up through my high range. How can that be Well, it takes two important things to accomplish this: a) know-how and b) muscular development. The latter of the two takes time. So, do not forget what I just said, "As you experiment with new things, constantly go back and be sure you can still do everything you were able to do before."

A reasonable question would be, "Why should we even consider mixing different schools of singing?" Well, there is a good rationale for this—so carefully consider the following: "Every solution has its problems."

Now, isn't that a Spoonerism? Didn't I mean to say, "Every problem has its solution?"

No, I meant *exactly* what I said! Each *particular technique* will bring with it some *particular limitation*. For example, you occasionally meet up with those rare male singers who have had glorious high voices from day-one. Such singers are often blessed with beautiful pianissimi in the high range and insist that singing up there is as easy, if not easier, than singing in the middle range. But most of them, great as they might have been, seem to have had one thing in common: middle voices that left a little bit to be desired, being on the nasal or muddy side.

In contrast, consider the more common case of those singers who have gorgeous middle voices, but obviously work a little harder for the high notes. They usually take it as axiomatic that singing in the high range requires more effort than singing in the middle range. I was one of those, but I eventually found it did not have to be so. Those singers with extraordinary high notes are not vocal freaks. An easy high voice can be acquired. Then there is the case of the singer with a brilliant projection in the middle and high range, who has a thin low voice. This is probably not something you are born with, but it is probably the result of your school of singing.

By contrast, there are singers who have extremely wide ranges and again we tend to consider them as freaks. Among baritones, where, outside of Leonard Warren, could you find such gorgeous high notes as Cornell MacNeal's? Yet Mac had a better low D than most bassos. Every time he sang the finale of the Rigoletto/Sparafucile duet with Norman Treigle at the New York City Opera, he would turn his back and sing the low F for Norman, who simply didn't have it.

Then there was Lauritz Melchior, the greatest of all Helden-tenors, who had a beautiful low C.

How to explain such anomalies? Is it just because we are all so differently endowed, or is it simply because we are each singing with a different vocal approach? I am convinced it is more the approach than endowment and if you sing the way Cornell MacNeal or Lauritz Melchior did, you too would probably have an extraordinary range.

In an effort to explain some of these anomalies, I will propose the controversial concept that all singers, male and female alike, have what I like to call four "voices." We will discuss this later in great detail. But, for now, it will suffice to say that a singer can utilize all of these "voices," a fact often ignored by those teachers who concentrate on exclusively using only one of them. They will require the student to carry a particular sound up or down throughout the entire range without resorting to any change in placement.

As an example, take the young singer who has a naturally thrilling high range, but a muddy middle-low range. The teacher says, "What you have in the high voice must be brought down to the middle. But don't let anything change as you do it." Actually, following this advice is what gives you that muddy middle voice. Ideally, the male singer's middle voice should be approached in a manner quite different from the way he approaches his high voice.

Now consider the case of the young singer with a naturally exciting middle voice who struggles for high notes. Then comes a similar admonition, "What you have in the middle voice, you must carry up to the top. But don't let anything change as you do it." A similar dilemma! You will achieve a reasonably good high voice, yet it will always be harder to produce than the middle—and this does not need to be so! The high voice should be as easy to produce as the middle.

Going from middle to high voice without any basic change in placement can be made to work, but never perfectly, since the high voice and the middle voice are two different entities—and that only accounts for two out of the four voices we males and females all possess. Ideally, these four voices should have four different placements, but the reality is that four different schools of singing have evolved out of exclusively using only one of them.

In the following chapters, we will discuss the four different voices possessed by both male and female singers, and how they are to be blended together to make what sounds to the ear as one.

We will also try to clarify some of the mystery that accompanies the essential, but nebulous terms commonly used by singers such as head voice, chest voice, etc.

And bear in mind that the vocal instruments used by men and women are not alien to each other. The human larynx for both sexes is anatomically the same, the only difference being the relative size of the components. By analogy, consider the contrast between the violin and the cello which, though similarly constructed and differing basically only in size, have to be played quite differently.

Regarding similarities, consider the woman's change of register from what they call "chest" to the "middle voice," which occurs somewhere just above middle C. This is exactly the same range where basses, baritones and tenors also have their main change of register. The basic difference is that men use their three lower voices on the stage and avoid singing in the highest female range (except for countertenors), while women use their three higher voices on the stage, and avoid singing in the lowest male range (except for "belting"). But we will discuss all of this later.

In closing, how can you be sure that what I am saying is valid? Well, bear in mind that I am not just presenting theory, but pragmatic experience. When teachers cannot demonstrate what they teach, they are presenting nothing more than "theories" or "opinions" which might or might not be valid. When they can actually practice what they teach, they are no longer talking "theory" but "demonstrable fact."

In other words, I will not suggest you do anything that I (now in my mid-seventies) cannot do myself. If anyone wishes to challenge me on these matters, I will simply suggest they meet me face to face and do with their voices the things I do with mine. In other words, let them "put up or shut up."

Now let us get on with it...

CHAPTER I

VOCAL AXIOMS

1) *"Support that tone!"*
2) *"Don't force!"*
3) *"If you breath correctly, you sing correctly."*
4) *"Breathing must be natural!"*
5) *"Sing with pear-shaped tones!"*
6) *"Sing easily!"*
7) *"Keep a square throat!"*
8) *"Sing on the breath, not with the breath!"* or,
   "Imagine a ball bouncing on top of a fountain!"
9) *"Sing exactly the same way as you speak!"*

These are just some of the clichés which every serious voice student will be subjected to sooner or later. And such statements seem to have a certain ring of truth—but do they, really?

Let us examine these clichés to see if they truly bear up under careful scrutiny.

It is not enough merely to memorize and spout vocal axioms: good singing is infinitely more than much talk and head-knowledge. The principle challenge of the student-teacher relationship is to translate certain verbal statements into body language. The student must learn to delicately monitor his/her internal physiological sensations and attempt to consistently reproduce those that create sounds acceptable to the teacher.

But there are two major handicaps in teaching a student to sing. One is that both pupil and teacher may have some misconceptions concerning the most commonly used terms such as "support," "appoggio," "diaphragm," "breath control," etc. The other handicap is to be found in the vocal axioms themselves, which often promise more than they can deliver, simply because they are not stated clearly.

1) Support that tone!

In the late forties, a young tenor debuted at the "Old Met" in a most challenging role and ran into a common problem that plagued even the most seasoned European artists when they first set foot in that giant house. It was very hard for the singers to hear themselves and they were prone to give too much, vocally. Our tenor's problem was compounded by the fact that he had not had one moment of rehearsal on the stage, since he was in the second cast. What a way to make a debut—but that was the way we American singers were treated in those days (I hope it has changed a bit since then, but I doubt it).

Halfway through the performance the hapless tenor cracked on one of the more difficult high notes. He returned into the wings totally demolished and our general manager, Edward Johnson, who himself had enjoyed a distinguished career as a leading tenor at the Met, confronted the dejected singer with,

"Support that tone, boy, support that tone!"

Our tenor then returned to the stage determined to redeem himself and, having a strong athletic physique, used all the formidable power of his muscular body to "support that tone" and cracked the next high note even worse. What Edward Johnson had in mind obviously had nothing to do with what the confused singer attempted on stage. Was it the tenor's fault? I think not! The fault probably lay in the wording of the cliché, "Support that tone!"

Fortunately, the story had a happy ending. Our tenor soon resolved the problem of his high notes by heeding the following advice given to him by Renato Cellini, then a coach on the Met staff:

"Take a strong laxative before you sing, and you won't dare force on your high notes!"

However indelicate it may be, this turned out to be much more useful than "Support that tone" and our young tenor quickly improved his high voice under the colorful tutelage of Maestro Cellini.

Let us take a good look at "Support that tone!" First of all, what is meant by the word "support"? The Merriam-Webster definition is "to hold up, or serve as a foundation for." Then one could logically ask, when speaking of "support," exactly what holds up what? Can a tone, which is a train of vibrations in the air, be held in any way, including "up," when it has neither mass, nor form, nor dimensions?

To further complicate the issue, the term Italians use in place of "support" is "appoggio," a noun derived from the verb "appoggiare," which means "to lean down upon." Are we then to infer that English speaking singers are to "hold up the tone" while their Italian colleagues are to "lean down upon it"? The English and Italian words seem to contradict each other.

Are you sufficiently confused, dear singer? Patience! The situation can be made excruciatingly worse by examining some of our other cliché axioms.

2) Don't force!

In my early years at the Met, I often dated the brilliant young coloratura soprano, Patrice Munsel, and our dinner conversations usually ended up sounding like vocal master-classes. Like all young, overworked prodigies at the Met, we were constantly showered with gems of wisdom from the self-appointed experts, and one of the most common admonitions we encountered was, "Don't force!"

"Don't force WHAT?" my vivacious partner slurred out one evening between mouthfuls of dinner salad. Her anguished question struck directly at the heart of the cliché's problem. Again we confront a statement that at first glance seems quite meaningful, but does not stand up too well under scrutiny.

"Don't force!" is a negative statement and negative statements have one drawback: while they tell you "what *not* to do," they fail to tell you "what *to* do." You don't learn to sing by *not doing*, but by *doing*! Naturally, if a singer has acquired bad habits, those habits should be eliminated. But how? By *not* doing something? Hardly. The only proper way to eliminate bad habits is to replace them with good ones.

The maxim "Don't force!" also raises another question: "What is the distinction between *force* and *strength*? After all, some muscular strength is required to produce the bigger than life sound of the operatic voice. By contrast, in singing circles "force" has all the connotations of a four-letter word. Let us try to resolve this problem by defining "*force*" as "strength misapplied." Does this help any? Not much.

We could interpret "strength misapplied" as too little or too much strength. But, how little or how much of a good thing does it take to be bad? For example, water is good to drink, but drink too much of it and you drown!

"Strength misapplied" could also be interpreted as use of the wrong muscles (another negative statement). Why should the use of certain muscles be regarded as "good" or "bad"? Do not all of the muscles of our bodies serve some good purpose?

In fact, we must even be careful how we use the terms "good" and "bad." Sand is good on a beach, but, bad in the crankcase of your car. Lead is good for the combustion of gasoline in your carburetor, but bad in your lungs. "Good" and "bad" are terms that only make sense when used with respect to a specific function.

To augment the confusion even more, let us skewer yet another of our cliché/axioms.

3) If you breathe correctly, you sing correctly!

Please, don't be led astray by the oversimplified notion that proper use of the breathing apparatus will magically provide a panacea for all your vocal problems. To say that vocal technique is nothing more than breath control is as foolish as saying that a steam locomotive is nothing more than a boiler. Obviously, a boiler is fundamental to the design and function of a steam locomotive, but the pressure generated in the boiler must be properly transmitted through the pistons to the axles and wheels. Just as a steam locomotive is "more than a boiler," so is a singer more than a "bellows in search of an audience."

Discussing proper use of the breath in singing is but a single facet of vocal technique. One must also acknowledge and study other facets such as "open throat" and "placement."

4) Breathing must be natural!

What could be less controversial than that? Well, let's zero in on this one and see if we can succeed in messing it up as thoroughly as we did the others.

What, then, is "natural" to homo sapiens in regard to breathing? Should we base our study of "natural breathing" upon some statistical study of how the average person breathes? Let's try that and see how far it gets us.

It is a statistical fact that a greater percentage of men breathe abdominally than do women. One would expect, then, to find male teachers leaning more heavily upon abdominal breathing than would woman teachers. In my experience, this seems to be exactly the case, so who is right—and what is natural—and for which sex?

Let us try another tack. We are often told that to understand natural breathing we should watch a baby crying in its crib. Of course, it is easy to see that its breathing is abdominal. Does that clinch it? Not quite. Statistical studies show that everyone tends to breathe more abdominally when in a prone position than when in a standing position. We usually observe a crying baby lying on its back, whereas, we usually observe opera singers standing on their feet (unless one's name is Magda Olivero). What, then, is natural and in what position?

To make things even more difficult, how can we relate the natural breathing of the average man to the natural breathing of the average opera singer, when the average man has never even tried to make an operatic sound? Opera singing is not something that comes naturally to the average man, so perhaps we are wrong to proceed in this direction.

May I propose that, instead of speaking about natural breathing, let us speak of proper breathing, or the type of breathing that would be most effective in producing good results over a long period of time, say, at least twenty or thirty years of professional vocal career.

5) Sing with pear-shaped tones!

Now, isn't that a cliché which is clear and self-explanatory? Let's see. Surely, everyone knows what a pear looks like—fat on the bottom and narrow at the top (I've known more than a few opera singers who also fit that description). The problem with trying to sing with pear-shaped tones is that no one ever bothers to tell you where the fat end of the pear is located. Does it lie in the front of the mouth or in the back? Or might it even be found down in the larynx? (Notice I am not saying that this cliché is worthless. On the contrary, I intend to use this particular type of imagery in a practical sense later on.)

But, please allow me the pleasure of cliché-bashing just a few more times and then we will shift from the destructive to the instructive.

6) Sing easily!

To a large extent, we have already touched upon vocal techniques related to this axiom. But, as I pointed out earlier, some sort of muscular strength is required in producing an operatic sound. So, just how easy should singing be?

In the fall of 1945, I sang Osmin in Mozart's *The Abduction from the Seraglio* in New Orleans. I became friendly with Charles Curtis who sang Pedrillo and he soon made it clear that he disapproved of my gutsy way of singing, maintaining he would never risk harming his God-given voice by forcing it like I did mine.

In 1946, he had a stage audition at the Met and was rejected because his voice was too small. It came as no surprise to me, since his whole philosophy was based upon "sing easily."

Six years later, he and I sang in *Faust* with the Florentine Opera in Milwaukee, but this time he displayed a surprisingly heroic voice. In changing his vocal approach, he had not resorted to force, but had found the secret of using properly controlled strength. Unfortunately Charlie died the year after and I feel the opera world lost a potentially fine talent. "Sing easily?" How easily can one sing and still be effective? How forcefully can one sing and still remain vocally healthy?

7) Keep a square throat!

This maxim was given to Rosa Ponselle by Enrico Caruso. Obviously he was trying to describe some sort of configurational setting in his throat which, considering the source, should be given serious attention. There is a little problem that complicates the discussion: is the square standing on end in the throat, or is it lying flat in the throat? Your guess is as good as mine. More about that later.

8) Sing on the breath, not with the breath! or,
Imagine a ball bouncing on top of a fountain!

I have combined these two axioms into one because they are so closely related.

Is the distinction between "on the breath" and "with the breath" quite clear to you? I must admit that for many years its meaning eluded me. We are told that "singing on the breath" is best

7

pictured as "a ball bouncing (or floating) on top of a fountain of water." Now that seems a bit clearer—except for one thing—just where are we supposed to imagine this "floating ball" to be located? Behind the upper teeth? Behind the eyeballs? Just over the vocal folds? Where, then? That leaves something to be said, doesn't it?

9) Sing exactly the same way as you speak!

This cliché is only applicable if the student has a natural, beautifully placed speaking voice. But, what does one do with those hordes of poor souls, including singers, who constantly consult speech therapists to correct bad habits acquired in early childhood. And, indeed, any laryngologist who treats opera singers can tell you that many successful performers who sing technically well constantly damage their vocal folds through poor speech habits. Singers with this sort of problem could profit by the reverse cliché/axiom, "Speak exactly the same way you sing."

A more accurate restatement of this would be, "Speak and sing in exactly the same way" (assuming, of course, that you do both correctly). Anyway, if you speak beautifully, emulate that in your singing—or, if you sing beautifully, emulate that in your speaking.

I have noticed that those who advocate this approach never seriously consider the fact that most of us breathe differently when we sing and when we speak. Be honest, now, do you take a breath before you speak? Of course not! You speak with the residual air already in your lungs; at the end of the phrase you relax and the elasticity of your system draws you back to the neutral, relaxed state from which you began.

But singers commonly take a breath before singing. There is contradiction between these two procedures and it must be resolved before one can honestly face this cliché. We will discuss this in depth in the chapter entitled "Support/Appoggio Revisited."

By now, irritated pedagogues reading this book might be saying, "Never mind statistics, everyone knows that breathing should be *natural-abdominal-diaphagmatic*" (whatever that is supposed to mean). The question really is, why should we challenge the value of these clichés handed down from generation to generation? Can we afford to blatantly ignore the lore left us by our predecessors? Surely, there have been many great singers and teachers in the past and we would be foolish to disregard their wisdom.

However, the issues raised in this chapter are ones that should be faced by any serious singer. Don't let it become a case of "What every singer should know but never bothered to ask." In my opinion, intelligent singers are the only ones to last for decades on the stage. This does not necessitate an academic or intellectual orientation, but does require an open, honest and inquiring mind.

What I call "The Trinity of Truth," Knowledge, Understanding and Wisdom never damaged anyone's career. The world of opera has grown too vast, too complex, too competitive for yesterday's uneducated, primitive type to survive for long. Today's performer can no longer afford to be musically illiterate or mentally indifferent. To succeed on the opera stage in this generation and to maintain a good level of success for many years requires a diligent development and application of all of one's resources.

If what I have written thus far has confused you, well and good! This confusion does not necessarily reflect any shortcoming on your part but, instead, reflects the deficiencies inherent in these cliché/axioms which are spouted by many teachers and singers.

However, we must not conclude that these maxims from the past are without any real value. Truth gleams out from them, much as precious gold gleams out from the crudest ore. We must attempt to refine that ore into a purer form; so let us now boldly enter the mysterious realm of "vocal art" with the intent of rendering it a bit more "sciency." It would be too narrow an approach for us to regard vocal technique as either "pure art" or "pure science." The two must be gracefully wedded into the Art/Science of singing.

CHAPTER II

SUPPORT/APPOGGIO

(Omit if desired, but you'll be sorry)

L et us begin our study of Support/Appoggio with a look at the anatomy of the human respiratory system. The breathing apparatus begins with the passageways of the nose and mouth which merge behind the tongue in the region called the naso-pharynx (*see Diagram 1, page 12*) and divide again into the alimentary and respiratory tracts.

The part of the alimentary tract in the chest is called the esophagus, which carries food and drink into the stomach. The beginning of the lower respiratory tract is called the trachea, which carries air from the larynx, or voice-box, and then splits into two tubes called the bronchi (*see Diagram 2, page 12*) which lead into the left and right lungs.

The lungs, together with the heart, are housed inside the rib-cage, a semi-rigid structure that resembles a bird cage and is composed of

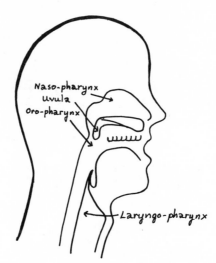

Diagram 1

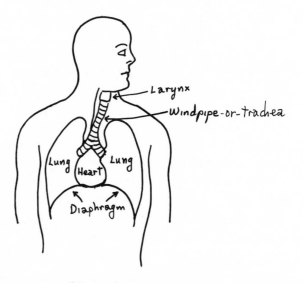

Diagram 2

ribs that are connected to each other by the intercostal muscles.

This cage can be expanded upward and outward, or contracted inward and downward. It can also be marginally raised and lowered by and with the shoulders.

The bottom, or floor, of the cage is a thin, muscular sheath with the shape of a double dome called the "diaphragm." Don't be misled by the ignoramus who pats his fat tummy and calls it his "diaphragm." That, instead, would be far better called a "poly*glut*" mass of lard and abdominal muscles. You are not likely to ever see a diaphragm with your naked eye unless you get your kicks by attending autopsies.

The diaphragmatic sheath is attached to the lower ribs of the rib-cage, circling from the front to the back of the trunk of the body, separating the chest cavity from the abdominal cavity. It bisects the trunk in a somewhat horizontal manner and, because of its double-domed shape, it could be said that we have two diaphragms, left and right. (*See Diagram 3.*)

The esophagus penetrates the diaphragm as it leaves the chest cavity and enters the abdominal cavity. It is securely seated at the point of penetration. When that ligamentous seal is torn, one suffers what is called a hiatus hernia.

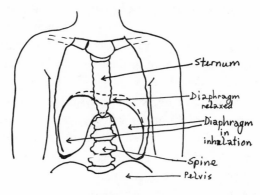

Diagram 3

13

Although the diaphragm is a very important factor in breathing, it is far from being the whole story. Other important muscles to be dealt with in breathing are the abdominals which include the external oblique, internal oblique, transversus abdominus and rectus abdominus. Secondary muscles of respiration are the internal and external intercostals, and the back and neck muscles. I will not provide a diagram for all the primary and secondary muscles of support since I do not feel it will make you sing any better. If you are curious about such things, there are many other books that go into great detail on the subject. I personally feel that too deep an anatomical approach only aggrandizes the author instead of serving the singer. Of course, no knowledge is ever wasted, but one can surely learn how to sing without knowing which muscle to twitch at which time.

Now that we have some idea about the anatomy of the breathing apparatus, let us see how it functions.

The lungs are spongy air sacs which, when filled with fresh air, transfer their oxygen into the bloodstream. At the same time, carbon dioxide, a by-product of body activity, is transferred from the bloodstream back into the air sacs in the lungs, to be expelled by exhalation. Homeostatic systems in the body direct the breathing process according to the levels of oxygen and carbon dioxide in the blood. The need for more oxygen causes a slight quickening of the breathing. On the other hand, an overt buildup of carbon dioxide in the blood initiates a more dramatic response typified by gasping for breath with violent heaving of the chest and shoulders. In real life this is usually caused by extreme physical activity such as vigorous running, jumping or swimming, where excessive amounts of carbon dioxide are produced in the cells and enter the bloodstream.

This type of exaggerated breathing is seldom seen in the performing arts, except in the case of strenuous dancing and would rarely, if ever, be seen in connection with operatic or concert performances. Singing requires considerable physical strength, but the breath should not be employed in such ferocious bursts that one's carbon dioxide level would rise sufficiently to cause gasping and chest heaving.

Now consider how the lungs are inflated and deflated. Among opera singers, the most commonly discussed part of the breathing apparatus is the diaphragm. It is hard to find a singer who does not profess to breathe "diaphragmatically," or "with the diaphragm." The diaphragm is often referred to as "the principle muscle of support."

THIS IS FALSE! (Unfortunately, we will have to deflate more than just lungs, but also a few misinformed vocal pedagogues.)

The diaphragm is involved in the process that is commonly called "support," but it is *not a muscle of support at all*! As we saw, the diaphragm is a double-domed sheath of muscle that arches up into the thoracic cavity when it is in the rest, or relaxed position. The only function of any muscle is to contract. When the diaphragm contracts, only one basic thing happens: it flattens out and if the rib-cage is kept more or less immobile, as in the case of gentle breathing, the diaphragm moves downward in the chest cavity, much like a piston. This initiates a sucking action in the chest cavity, producing what is commonly called "negative pressure," drawing air into the lungs through the remainder of the respiratory tract. Therefore the diaphragm, which can only contract and relax, is primarily *instrumental in inhalation*.

"Support" is something called into action only during a particular kind of exhalation which requires a more forceful expulsion of breath, such as is needed in singing. It is not required for gentle breathing. We humans are not like birds which sing both on exhalation and inhalation; we only sing as we exhale. If the diaphragm is not a muscle of exhalation, how, then, does it enter into the so-called support of vocal sound? To answer this, we must first understand how the muscles controlling exhalation interact with those controlling inhalation.

Muscles which manipulate the bony structures of the body are called "skeletal" muscles. This, of course, excludes heart muscles, sphincters, peristaltic muscles, etc. As a general rule, any contraction of a skeletal muscle is accompanied by the simultaneous contraction of an opposing skeletal muscle.

15

If, for example, I wish to raise my hand to my face by bending my elbow, I contract my biceps. My triceps contract at the same time, countering the motion. Naturally, for my hand to actually make the move toward my face, the biceps must override the triceps. To bring my hand back down, the triceps must override the biceps.

Why this pitting of one muscle against the other? Isn't it a waste of energy? No, it is Nature's way of giving you smooth, controlled motion. If the biceps contracted without the opposing control of the triceps, your hand would fly up and hit you in the face. This is the way all of the skeletal muscles behave, with two major exceptions—the diaphragm under certain circumstances—and the abdominals, under others.

In normal, gentle breathing, as the diaphragm contracts, causing inhalation, it meets an elastic resistance from various sources. The lungs are somewhat elastic, and strive, much like an air-filled balloon, to return to the neutral position. The liver, and possibly other organs, are displaced from their normal positions, also adding to the elastic tension. And, most importantly, the abdominal cavity is stretched downward and outward, adding to the eventual elastic recoil. We must also note that the diaphragm itself elastically tends to return to its original dome shape. All of these elastic factors combined are sufficient, in gentle breathing, to provide the necessary controlling counterforce for the diaphragm.

But, taking a gentle, shallow breath and allowing the elastic forces to produce the exhalation do not constitute what is commonly meant by support, nor can one produce a strong, focused tone by such a mild exhalation. Of course, sound can be produced by this sort of relaxed exhalation, but this is generally regarded as an "unsupported tone." In this relaxed form of inhalation/exhalation, first the diaphragm contracts, met by the elastic forces which grow as the inspiration continues. Then the diaphragm begins to relax until the elastic forces predominate, at which time exhalation begins. Little by little the diaphragm further relaxes until it returns to its upper position. Generally, both the contractual force of the diaphragm and the elastic forces are constantly pitted against each other, providing smooth, controlled breathing.

When a stronger exhalatory force is required in order to shout or sing with operatic intensity, the *support* muscles must come into play. For the moment, let us disregard the intercostal muscles (the muscles between the ribs) and consider the principle muscles of support: the abdominals.

After a deep inhalation, were one to completely relax the diaphragm and at the same time employ a strong contraction of the abdominals, there would result an uncontrolled ejection of air which would be far too violent for good singing. Instead, the diaphragm must provide the controlling counterpressure for the abdominals, otherwise the only other means of controlling the resulting violent air flow would be to precipitately close the vocal folds on each attack: a most effective means of prematurely ending a vocal career.

It is this controlled use of *strength* and *counterstrength* that underlies the concept of Support/Appoggio. "Support," or "holding up," is provided by the abdominals. "Appoggio," or "leaning down upon," is provided by the diaphragm. One is essential to the controlled function of the other. To speak of "support" without including "appoggio" generally gives an incomplete picture of reality. For this reason, we shall refer to the more complete concept of Support/Appoggio.

We have somewhat oversimplified our discussion of the breathing apparatus by ignoring the influence of the intercostal and back muscles. The intercostals can increase and decrease the volume of air used in breathing by expanding and contracting the rib-cage. The external intercostal muscles increase the size of the rib-cage, and the internal intercostal muscles decrease its size. In a limited way, the back muscles have some effect on inhalation and exhalation. Although some singers utilize a tightening of the gluteal muscles of the buttocks, these muscles have no direct effect on expansion and contraction of the lungs and rib-cage.

Well, can we expect this meander through the fields of anatomy

17

and Support/Appoggio to afford you a great breakthrough in your singing? I sincerely doubt it, since it only represents a part of the picture. As I said earlier, "Good singing is *infinitely* more than much talk and head-knowledge." So, let us take one more finite step into that seemingly infinite and mysterious realm of good singing.

Chapter III

Support / Appoggio
Revisited

(To be read—or else!)

In this chapter, we will now use the singer's approach to breathing rather than the anatomist's and try to be more "arty" than "sciency."

After reading the previous chapter you might object that the study of singing should not be so mechanical. However, one cannot escape the fact that we sing with a marvelously constructed machine. But since I am a God-fearing man, I will not restrict myself to a narrow, mechanistic view of the human frame.

Therefore I will resurrect that troublesome word, "natural." Most people feel it deserves a place of respect in our vocal vocabulary and so do I, despite the way I tried to do it in a while ago. If we human beings could revert to an Edenic existence where man, created in perfection and living in an ideal state of communion with his Creator, had not succumbed to the temptation to eat of the fruit of

"The Tree of Knowledge of Good and Evil," it would not be necessary to learn anything: it would all come naturally.

But we have eaten of the "forbidden fruit" and, like it or not, we must now struggle to obtain knowledge of right and wrong. But, there are vestiges of the "natural" in all of us, so we are capable of doing some things instinctively without resorting to logic's cumbersome procedures. It boils down to right brain versus left brain: intuition versus logic. We have no choice but to live with this state of affairs and try to utilize the best of both alternatives.

A word of warning: one occasionally meets a singer who claims to have had it all "naturally" from the beginning, maintaining he or she never had a need for a voice teacher. And in my experience these natural singers are often very exciting performers, but they usually prove to be the most vulnerable. Heaven help them if, after ten or fifteen years in the profession, they bump their noses on challenging roles. Should they crash, and they often do, they usually stay crashed because these natural singers, never having learned how to use their voices in the first place, haven't the foggiest notion of what to do when problems arise!

Ideally, teachers should try to give their pupils a complete understanding of what they should be doing. But the common practice is to first ascertain how much a pupil can do instinctively and then not tamper with whatever comes naturally. The teacher usually fills in the gaps, applying reasoning only when intuition is not sufficient. When a snag is discovered, it is approached through reasoning or imagery, and when the solution is found, the student is encouraged to remember and re-employ the body sensations that accompany it until they become automatic or "natural."

When my first teacher, Gennaro Curci, approached the subject of breathing, he said it should be as natural as possible. Since I showed no initial signs of difficulty, he did not dwell on the subject. But that only sufficed to get me through the first seven years.

My first major problem came from singing at the Old Met. The high-domed horseshoe design of the auditorium, with its back wall literally a city block away, was an intimidating sight from the stage. I had already performed in larger theaters than that venerable hall, but the Old Met had rather treacherous acoustics: while the audience could hear you perfectly, you could hardly hear yourself! The most common advice one encountered was "Don't force!"

A host of singers, including some highly ballyhooed foreign "superstars," made pretty sad debuts at the Old Met. The most common symptom was insecurity in the high notes. When Maria Callas came to the Met, even she developed problems with her—up to then—phenomenal high voice. So, when my high notes began to betray me, I had plenty of company.

One of my audition pieces at the Met was the Monologue from *Boris Godunov.* For the first time in five years on the professional stage, my high notes gave me trouble: I felt a scratch on the high G-flats. However, I seemed to be the only one that noticed it, since I was handed a lucrative contract the next day.

But even if my problem was not particularly audible, I was intensely aware of it. The singer is usually the first to know when something is wrong. So when it comes to trouble shooting, the way the voice *feels* is as important as how it *sounds.*

Several months later, I debuted at the Met and within a short time performed the role of Mephistopheles in *Faust,* a part which I had done extensively in other major theaters. That is when my troubles really began and any note over D above middle C became scratchy and insecure.

I struggled with that handicap for three interminable years and got away with it, even drawing excellent reviews. But I wasn't fooling myself; I knew I was in trouble. When a change of voice teachers didn't help, I began to suspect I was born with a *short voice,* a voice which was, by nature, hopelessly incapable of spanning a full two octave range.

In my fourth year at the Met, I was assigned the role of Dossife in *Khovanschina.* I went into shock when I saw the unbelievable number of high notes to be sung by "yours truly" and knew there was no way I was going to sing that role without a miraculous change in my technique. Indeed, up to the day of the final dress rehearsal, I did not once sing the entire role in full voice. Not only was I psyched out, I simply did not have the vocal know-how to meet the challenge.

The miracle I needed came in the person of Kurt Baum, who was at that time the Met's reigning "King of the High C." I ran into him at the stage door on the day of the dress rehearsal and in sheer desperation, I asked him what I was doing wrong. He insisted my problem with the high voice came from misuse of the breath, saying, "The higher you go the deeper you must feel your 'appoggio.' As you sing higher, you must take the breath pressure away from your vocal cords. Drink the tone. On a high C, I almost feel like I'm inhaling instead of exhaling. You must support deeper as you sing higher."

The message was loud and clear: the time had come for me to start giving serious thought to the concepts of *support* and *appoggio*. And that very morning I made a quantum leap in my understanding of the use of the breath. What I had tried to do naturally in the past simply was not enough for the job. Yes, I found the miracle I so desperately needed and performed the role of Dossife quite successfully.

"Appoggio" became an integral part of my vocabulary, and I mean a real "low-down appoggio"—the pushing down in the abdomen that is described as the feeling of "giving birth to a baby" (why we men so commonly use this analogy is a mystery—what do we know about giving birth to a baby?), or sometimes less delicately described as "going to the bathroom." (Now that is a subject on which all of us can speak with authority.)

However described, a more proper use of the breath furnished me with new and valuable insights. But helpful as it was, this approach did not solve all my problems, since it also helped me develop an inguinal hernia (which, by the way, is quite common among male opera singers, including my late colleague, Kurt Baum).

Thus my first encounter with appoggio ended up a mixed blessing.

Since that time, I have learned that there are several different, yet viable ways of approaching Support/Appoggio, all of which are well worth our attention

First of all, what is the objective of Support/Appoggio? It has to do with delivering sufficient pressure of breath against the vibrating vocal folds to produce a strong, healthy sound, yet *without overdoing it.* If a singer uses too much breath pressure while placing the voice in the mask, the edges of the vocal folds can begin to uncontrollably slip apart as the strained laryngeal muscles go into spasms. The result is a scratchy sound, or outright cracking into the falsetto. That, in fact, accounts for my earlier experience with unstable high notes.

Sufficient breath pressure to sustain an operatic sound is provided by the abdominal support muscles, augmented, in some approaches, by the intercostals and back muscles. The basic controlling force that prevents excessive pressure is provided by the diaphragm, aided in some cases by the outer intercostal muscles. Now what does that mean?

Let us begin by considering the low Support/Appoggio upon which we touched earlier. By this approach, the breath is taken deep in the abdominal region with no involvement of the rib-cage, the chest remaining static. Then the force needed for exhalation is provided by a contraction of all the support muscles around the abdominal cavity, beginning just below the ribs. The feeling is one of pushing down from all around the lower trunk of the body. It is the typical *straining* of *birth* or *bathroom.*

Using the imagery of "drawing the sound out of the throat," sometimes described as "drinking the tone," prompts the diaphragm to more strongly resist the support muscles. This concept is especially important when approaching the high voice. As one ascends in pitch, the vocal folds increasingly draw closer together, causing a build up of pressure from below. "Drinking the tone" counters the instinct to pit more breath pressure against the vocal folds on high notes. Withholding pressure helps one to avoid

23

gripping the high notes, allowing them to come out full and relaxed.

A common cliché used in conjunction with this type of Support/Appoggio is "think deeper as you sing higher" (in this case, the word "deeper" applies as much to the abdominal region as it does to the laryngeal). As I have already noted, the major drawback to this approach is the increased risk of an inguinal hernia in male singers.

A second type of Support/Appoggio, sometimes described as "the balloon in the stomach," involves taking a breath much in the same manner as in the previous method. But, when the support muscles come into play, the general feeling is that of pressing in upon a balloon from all directions, around, above—and below. Pressing from below gives the feeling of a floor beneath the balloon which eliminates the sensation of straining down. In this type of exhalation the rib-cage is basically left out of it. The stomach muscles, just below the front of the rib-cage, bulge out a bit and the abdominal muscles, just below them, pull in.

This bulging out of the stomach muscles is often used to demonstrate what is sometimes called "singing diaphragmatically." One famous vocalist purportedly would lean his body against the piano and then forcefully shove it away by protruding this "balloon in the stomach." Such an approach to Support/Appoggio may possibly eliminate some of the risk of male singers incurring inguinal hernias, but that is only conjecture on my part.

Another method of breathing was brought to my attention by my third and last voice teacher, Samuel Margolis, a method he called "Yoga Breathing." The inhalation begins with the lower abdomen, then the stomach region begins to protrude, followed by an expansion of the lower rib-cage. There is absolutely no involvement of the upper chest and shoulders, which remain down as though one were wearing a yoke. This inhalatory action travels upward in a continuous wave motion until the lungs are sufficiently full to begin the phrase. When the expansion is completed, the rib-cage momentarily pauses in its expanded position while the exhalation begins in the lower abdomen. As the lower abdomen pulls in, the wave motion continues upward with a contraction in the stomach region, followed by a contraction of the rib-cage. The entire effect should be that of a continuous two phase cycle: a phase of inhalation, followed by a phase of exhalation, with each phase beginning in the lower abdomen, then spreading smoothly upward and ending with the lower rib-cage.

The three methods of Support/Appoggio just described are more commonly employed by men than by women. Women generally employ a higher position of breathing, which some attribute to the practice of wearing tight corsets in the last century, which prevented them from using the abdominal approach. I am not impressed by this argument. As I pointed out earlier, women generally tend to breathe less abdominally than do men. I can't see the logic of how this could be an inherited hangover from the "corset generation."

A fourth method, more commonly employed by women, starts with an inhalation involving a simultaneous expansion in the stomach region and the lower rib-cage, consequently drawing the back muscles into play and, in most cases, with very little involvement of the abdominals. As the exhalation begins, one maintains the outward stretch of the lower rib-cage, resisting its natural tendency to move inward with the deflation of the lungs. Although this method is more commonly employed by women, some prominent male singers also advocate its use.

At this point, it behooves me to touch upon a strange phenomenon that, with rare exception, exclusively plagues women. This common defect, found among many successful female singers, is the chin wobble, which becomes so pronounced at times that it becomes quite obvious in the sound produced.

Since Marilyn Horne has not the slightest trace of this defect, I once asked her what she thought was its cause. Her answer was a firm "lack of support." I know, from private discussion, that Marilyn advocates a low, abdominal approach. The fact that more males tend to use a lower form of Support/Appoggio than women, and the fact that they are almost never plagued by this problem, makes me think Marilyn is right. This is a subject worth investigating in depth.

Now consider a fifth and rather intriguing approach to Support/Appoggio which will be quite thought-provoking. I first encountered this challenging method when studying with my second teacher, Rocco Pandiscio, an Italian-trained baritone who sang extensively in the United States. The rationale of his method is a bit involved, but well worth the trouble of studying it.

This approach will force us to seriously consider the cliché/axiom "Sing exactly as you speak." As was the case with the other maxims we previously devastated, this one had basic flaws. As we stated, "This cliché is only applicable if the student has a natural, beautifully placed speaking voice."

There is one aspect of normal speech to which we must pay special attention: in ordinary conversation *one does not take a breath before speaking*. Think about that! You do not inhale and then say, "Hello, how are you?" You begin speaking while your breathing apparatus is in *a relaxed, neutral position*. When you finish a spoken phrase, you relax again and elastic forces automatically return you to the neutral position with no effort on your part. (This is the second exception to the rule that all skeletal muscles operate in opposing pairs, as discussed in the previous chapter. Here the skeletal muscles are controlled entirely by elastic forces.) The inhalation, then, is caused by a relaxation, whereas inhalation in the more common methods of singing described before, is produced by contraction of the diaphragm—a muscular action, not a relaxation!

This is obviously a type of breathing we have not previously touched upon. Quiet breathing associates inhalation with tensing of the diaphragm, and exhalation with its relaxation. But, in speaking, we have a contrary action: exhalation is associated with a tensing of the abdominal muscles of support and inhalation with their relaxation. So here we find something new and challenging: it would seem that the way we use our breathing muscles in normal speech is different from the way we commonly use them in singing.

We see, then, it would be impossible to sing and speak in exactly the same manner unless one were to use the breath in singing in the same manner as in speaking. That means starting each singing phrase without taking a breath! Is such a thing feasible? Is there a great enough volume of residual air in the lungs to sustain the average singing phrase?

See how long you can speak without first taking a breath. You will probably find you can go about fifteen seconds. Beginning with this same quantity of air, how long would you be able to sing? The question is: which actually requires the greater quantity of air, speaking or singing?

Try the classical experiment of speaking normally while holding a lighted candle about five inches before your lips. The flame will probably flicker, or even blow out. Relight the candle, and return it to the same position. Now produce a well-placed singing sound. This time, the flame should barely flicker (If it markedly flutters, do something practical like finding a new teacher). This experiment shows that you are using a smaller quantity of air in singing than in speaking, which is the result of properly manipulating your vocal folds.

The perfect analogy for this manipulation is found in using a garden hose without a nozzle. When you turn it on full strength, the water projects no more than two or three feet. If you press your thumb over the open end of the hose, the water squirts considerably further—and with much greater force. Did the amount of water flow increase? No, it probably decreased a bit. The difference lay in how you utilized the pressure.

When you sing, the closing of the vocal folds makes the difference, not the quantity of air in your lungs. Now, if the quantity of air used in singing is less than that used in speaking, and if you can speak for fifteen seconds without taking a breath, surely you can sing at least that long, or longer. Consider Diagram 1 (*page 28*):

Diagram 1

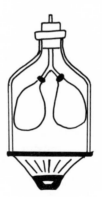

Diagram 2

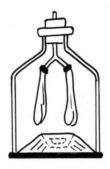

Diagram 3

The tube running through the cork at the top represents the trachea, or wind pipe. Where it branches out at the Y is the beginning of the two bronchial tubes, and the two balloons represent the lungs. A rubber diaphragm, stretched across the open bottom of the bell jar, represents, in a somewhat simplistic manner, the human diaphragm (simplistic, since the human diaphragm is not flat, but arched up into the chest cavity when in the relaxed, rest position). Bearing this in mind, the bell jar affords us a reasonable facsimile of the human breathing apparatus.

The two balloons in the rest position contain a certain amount of residual air, as do the lungs. To verify this, try exhaling from the rest position and you will see that a fair quantity of air is still available. In fact, in normal breathing we do not exchange more than 15-25 percent of the air in our lungs.

Glued onto the bottom of the rubber diaphragm of the bell jar is a handle, so it can be properly manipulated. If we pull down on the handle, stretching the membrane (*see Diagram 2, page 28*), air sucks in through the tube in the cork in the same manner that contraction of the human diaphragm sucks air into our lungs through the windpipe. This action inflates the balloons. Obviously, as we release the handle, it is the elasticity that pulls the diaphragm back to its initial position, deflating the balloons. This is a rough parallel to normal, quiet breathing.

It can be a different story, however, when we speak. To demonstrate this, we would have to push up on the handle, stretching the rubber diaphragm up into the bell jar, forcing the residual air out of the balloon (*see Diagram 3, page 28*).

This is how exhalation is accomplished in normal speech.

Then, to inhale, we simply release the membrane from below. In speaking or singing without taking a breath the support, or abdominal muscles, force the diaphragm upward into the chest cavity, an action which it resists by its contractility. When you relax the support muscles the diaphragm effortlessly drops back down to the neutral position.

In a sense, you don't take the breath, it is taken for you. The sensation is one of relaxation, rather than that of a muscular effort. Therefore the attack in each phrase is preceded by a sensation of relaxation, rather than tension. This is in direct contrast to the common mode of breathing used in singing in which the breath is taken by a muscular contraction of the diaphragm and the attack is preceded by tension between the diaphragm and the abdominal muscles.

The idea of attacking each singing phrase in a state of total relaxation is an appealing one because it allows the entire vocal apparatus to begin in a quiescent state. This way every attack can have a featherlight beginning and there is much less chance of abusing the vocal folds.

In the common mode of inhaling before singing, the diaphragm contracts, drawing in the breath, a process that is resisted by the elastic forces we discussed previously. As the phrase begins with exhalation, the diaphragm begins— I repeat —*begins* to relax. So, can we say the phrase begins easily because of this relaxation? No! The diaphragm is not relaxed at the beginning of the phrase, it is only beginning to relax. It will not be totally relaxed until the very end of the phrase, since it must act as a control against the elastic recoil and the support muscles.

So the attack is initiated with a high degree of oppositional force. As long as all the muscles involved are fresh, and can delicately counterbalance each other, the attack with the vocal folds can likewise be featherlight. But, when the diaphragm begins to tire at the end of a long performance, the combined forces of elastic recoil and support muscles tend to overwhelm the diaphragm on the attacks and they tend to become increasingly harsh. When the opposing forces involved are no longer in delicate balance, the air in the lungs is more forcibly expelled, prompting more abrupt and forcible closure of the vocal folds. That can only mean trouble.

If, instead, one sings without taking a breath, no matter how fatigued the breathing muscles become, every attack will still be gentle. That is the major advantage of this method. Most singers, when they first attempt it, have a panicky feeling that they are running out of breath and a fluttering sensation begins in the stomach, much the same sensation one gets when swimming a fair distance underwater. The problem is easily overcome with the confidence that comes with practice and experience.

There is a sixth variation on Support/Appoggio, practiced by both male and female singers. When one is singing in the higher range, the lower ribs are held higher, and the abdomen is lower. As one descends in range, the lower ribs descend, and the abdomen feels higher. It is a "bellows" type of situation, where one becomes conscious of the sensation of spacing between the bottom of the rib-cage, and the floor of the abdomen. The space between them is greater on high notes, and less on low. I suppose this technique can be practiced until it is automatic, but to a beginner it could be somewhat complex and even confusing.

A seventh approach to the way of taking and utilizing the breath also holds promise. One takes the breath by concentrating on exclusively expanding the abdominal region laterally. The sides of the torso under the rib-cage literally expand outward. Maintaining that feeling of low, lateral expansion all during the singing phrase distinctly helps in holding back excessive pressure from the vocal folds. Miguel Sanchez Moreno, the tenor that introduced me to this idea, came from the Melocchi School of singing, a method that requires a very strong use of appoggio, without which the vocal folds could be seriously damaged by the formation of nodes. We will discuss this further in the chapter on vocal health and trauma.

There is an eighth way of using the breath in singing which I will only touch upon here, but which I will explain in greater detail in the chapter on the use of the larynx. Here, the breath is blown through the vocal folds in an exaggerated form of crooning and one can use the full power of the support muscles without any resort to appoggio with the diaphragm. In fact, the only sensation of appoggio, or "leaning down," is in the region of the vocal folds.

31

This method seems to be "all support" and "no appoggio" in the common sense and can only be safely used if one does not attempt to "place" the tone in any way. There is no inherent danger to the delicate vocal folds, since this approach furnishes an ample cushion of air between them.

Finally, there is an approach which I definitely do not recommend, nor do most successful singers. It is a method of breathing which has been associated with ballet dancers. In addition to expanding the stomach region, together with the lower rib-cage and the back, the upper rib-cage is also expanded by raising the shoulders.

This inhalatory action reminds me of my college days when, after a strenuous run around the track, our coach would tell us to raise our arms above our heads to get a greater volume of air in our lungs. This was to help expel the excessive carbon dioxide which had reached high levels in our blood due to the strenuous activity.

All well and good for track stars and ballet dancers, but for singers I cannot advocate breathing which involves raising of the shoulders and upper chest. There is simply too great an elastic tension to be dealt with in this method, giving rise to a pronounced tendency to indulge in harsh vocal attacks at the beginning of each phrase. This can seriously damage those delicate folds, leading to the risk of polyps, nodes and other vocal trauma.

I strongly recommend avoiding any involvement of the upper chest and shoulders in singing. Leave the heave to runners, jumpers and swimmers. Obviously, this method provides a greater volume of air for the lungs, but good singing is not based upon using a great volume of air, but an efficient use of it. However, that also is the subject for another chapter.

No matter which of the above techniques you choose, it is important that the breath be used sparingly, and in such a manner that the vocal folds are treated gently. How is this accomplished? We must return to the unanswered questions of "How much strength and counterstrength should be applied?", "How little or how much of a good thing is needed to be bad?" and "Which of the methods described above is best for you, and under what circumstances?"

Heed the advice Bob Merrill gave me early in my career, "Sing with only 90 percent of your voice; never give it all!"

If you feel like you are weight lifting when you sing, it is wrong! Back off until the voice is floating and easy.

The resolution to all of these questions is to simply get a good teacher; because you will most likely never find the answers to all of these questions by merely reading a book. Even this book!

CHAPTER IV

TONGUE, JAW, LIPS, ET AL.

In addition to the breathing apparatus, the vocal apparatus also consists of the tongue, the naso-pharynx, the jaw, the soft and hard palates, the mouth, the lips, the sinuses and the larynx. We will now study the basic functions of these components, with the exception of the larynx, which is the prime subject of Chapter V.

Some of these components can be manipulated at will, others cannot. The tongue, for example, can be raised, lowered, curled, twisted, flattened or grooved. Such manipulations can be carried out either in a relaxed manner, or with muscular tension (which is undesirable).

The naso-pharynx is essentially the back of the throat, which includes the soft palate and uvula. It can be manipulated to independently raise the soft palate, but can also be manipulated to spread the rear walls of the mouth laterally as at the end of a yawn (a position that is definitely undesirable for good singing).

The jaw can be opened and closed, as well as moved forward and backward. These manipulations can be carried out with complete relaxation or with an accompanying muscular tension (another undesirable).

The lips can be pursed, protruded, spread wide or gathered together. These mannerisms may be employed at will (but are not necessary for good singing).

The other components cannot be manipulated, namely the hard palate, the teeth and the sinuses.

Of all the components of the vocal apparatus, only the larynx is capable of producing sound: the others only alter the quality of the sound the larynx produces. A simple experiment will give us a clue as to how this alteration is effected.

When I was a child, we played "Cowboys and Indians," putting our hands to our mouths and flapping them back and forth, making an "Indian Warwhoop." This simple "Warwhoop" is going to demonstrate a basic lesson in the physics of sound.

Try a little experiment. With the heel of your hand on your jaw and cheek, and with the hand extending out from your face, start singing an "ah" vowel. Then slowly move your whole hand to lie flat across your mouth. If you do this correctly, the vowel changes first to an "oh" and then to an "oo". If you reverse the procedure, the vowel returns through "oh" to "ah".

If you repeat this experiment starting with the vowel "eh" instead of "ah", you will pass through "ey" to "ee".

So, based upon the two vowels, "ah" and "eh", you can produce the entire spectrum of the six basic Italian vowels.

You should also repeat this experiment using your telephone as the transmitter. Pick up the handset and listen to the "aaa" sound coming from the earphone. Now flap your hand over the earphone just as you did with your mouth and listen to how the sound goes back and forth from "*aaa*" to "*oo*".

Using the telephone's earphone demonstrates that it is definitely not necessary to make any change in the transmitter (either the larynx or the earphone) to produce a change in the vowel sound; the only action required on your part is the motion of your hand and wrist. The vowel automatically changes according to the angle your hand makes with regard to your face or the earphone.

In each of these experiments the transmitter did not change— only the angle made by your hand changed. This reflection of the sound waves by your hand not only altered the direction in which the sound waves were traveling, but *altered the vowel as well.* But how does the reflecting of sound waves change the vowel sound?

Actually, vowel sounds are the mind's interpretation of what the physicist calls "phase difference." Understanding "phase difference" is not going to make you sing better, but if you are interested in knowing what it's all about you can refer to the Appendix.

It can be effectively demonstrated that one can go from any particular vowel sound to any other by simply changing the path that the sound waves take. The vowel changes are not produced by the transmitter (the larynx), but by the physiological components that can be manipulated to change the path of the vibrating column of air.

The tongue, the jaw, the naso-pharynx, the soft palate and the lips are the elements that work together to produce variations in vowel sound. The important fact to consider is that *these components only provide diverse pathways and have nothing to do with producing the sound.* This means that the muscular strength necessary for producing an operatic sound has nothing to do with any of these components. Only the larynx can produce sound. For example, when a certain position of the jaw is used to form a specific vowel, it is not necessary to employ some sort of force or strength to achieve that setting.

Make some particular vowel sound. Now tense the muscles of the jaw without changing its position in any way. If you do exactly as directed, there will be absolutely no change in the sound. It is the position of the jaw that counts, not some kind of muscular effort. Any such effort is *wasted* and the same applies to manipulations of

37

the tongue, lips and naso-pharynx. Only the shapes and positions of these components affect the sound, not muscular tensions.

The point I am trying to make is that any muscular tension employed in manipulating the tongue, jaw, lips and naso-pharynx is not only unnecessary, but undesirable. If you cannot produce all vowels throughout your entire vocal range without facial contortions and visible effort, then you are singing incorrectly!

Once you have set the positions of these components to make a particular vowel sound, going up and down throughout your entire range should require no further changes in position, that is if you are singing correctly. Contrary to popular opinion, the only necessary changes in going up and down in pitch are within the larynx, which produces the sound.

The idea that one cannot sing high notes without an increased opening of the jaw is totally false! Just because some people cannot do it, does not mean no one can. It is like a person on crutches insisting that everybody should use them!

If, for example, you sing an ascending scale beginning with the vowel "ee" on the lowest note in your range and go up to your highest note, it should not be necessary to make any change what-soever in the positions of the jaw, tongue, lips or naso-pharynx during the entire procedure.

I am aware it is often recommended that a singer open the jaw a little wider when ascending to the high notes. This is called "modifying the vowel," which is something one can choose to do as a matter of taste, *but it should not be a necessity.* For example, if a pure "ee" vowel is modified to "ih" on a high note, it should be a matter of choice, again not dire necessity. One should be able to produce a pure, unmodified "ee" vowel in any part of the range desired, but it will tend to have a somewhat sharp, unpleas-ant sound in the high voice. To make it more acceptable for the stage, it can be modified in ways other than just opening the jaw wider with ascending pitch. But more about that in Chapter VII on the "first-voice."

Further analysis of how to deal with the larynx, tongue, naso-pharynx, jaw, soft and hard palates, mouth, lips and sinuses will be pursued in subsequent chapters.

And the next time someone says "Don't force," recall this discussion, and use it to avoid "strength misapplied."

CHAPTER V

THE LARYNX

The larynx is whimsically referred to as the "Adam's Apple." So, to be "politically correct" and give the ladies their due, we will henceforth dub it the "Adam's/Eve's Apple." Let us now analyze the fruitful functioning of this essential vocal component as the subject of our present chapter.

Superficially, it would seem enough has been said concerning the use of the breath in the chapters on Support/Appoggio. But, if we were to neglect the involvement of the larynx in controlling the breath, it would be as foolish as neglecting to use a nozzle on a hose when watering the lawn. As I said in our discussion concerning vocal clichés, a singer is "more than a bellows in search of an audience." Let us pursue the analogy of the garden hose and nozzle a bit further.

A garden hose connected to a faucet usually has a nozzle to control how far the water will spurt. Without a nozzle the stream of water leaving the hose would only reach about two or three feet, which would be ineffective for watering a lawn or a garden. Adjusting the nozzle of the hose alters the aperture through which the water flows. Closing it a little compresses the water, which then squirts further. However, closing it to the extreme reduces the flow of water to a fine spray.

Just as the faucet supplies the driving force of the water, so do the support muscles supply the driving force of the breath with the larynx acting as the nozzle. Now the manner in which the larynx is used is critical because its misuse can cause severe and even permanent damage to the vocal folds.

Just as narrowing the aperture of the nozzle causes a backup of pressure in the hose, so does increasingly tighter approximation of the vocal folds cause a backup of pressure in the windpipe. While narrowing the aperture between the vocal folds produces a more brilliant and desirable sound, an excessive buildup of pressure, caused by squeezing the folds too tightly together, subjects them to an abrasive action which should be avoided like the plague.

To further complicate the situation, as one sings higher in pitch the vocal folds draw closer together causing an even greater buildup of pressure. How, then, is one to avoid potential damage?

As a start, let us agree that to protect the delicate vocal folds, any attack in a singing phrase should be gentle.

But reflect a moment—is not the term "attack" itself a poor choice of words? Does it not imply an aggressive act which in no way seems gentle? This word, unfortunately, is so deeply enshrined in the traditional terminology of singing that it would be almost impossible to eliminate its usage. So let us continue to employ it, but with the understanding that all "attacks" should somehow be gentle.

A natural question immediately comes to mind. Is it possible for a fortissimo attack to be gentle? Recall our discussion in the previous chapter which dealt with singing only on residual air, mandating that one should not take a breath before phonation. With such an approach one could ideally start each phrase with the vocal apparatus in a state of total relaxation. Then a fortissimo attack could be kept gentle for at least the first critical instant of phonation.

However, the more common approach is to take a breath before the attack, but then the diaphragm must be so carefully pitted against the support muscles, and so delicately balanced, that the larynx can always be in a completely relaxed state at the beginning of every phrase.

Such a situation would be comparable to having the faucet turned off, with the pressure still in the pipes, but not in the hose. Turning the faucet on but slightly is equivalent to letting the support muscles overcome the diaphragm sufficiently to initiate a gentle flow of air. The passing breath initiates the attack and the larynx comes into play as the nozzle.

Without going too deeply into the anatomy of the larynx, let us discuss some of the ways the vocal nozzle can be used. First of all, blowing air through an excised larynx produces an unimpressive buzzing sound. Resonances in the various cavities of the throat, naso-pharynx and mouth give rise to the sounds associated with speaking and singing.

As we noted in the previous chapter, the positions taken by the jaw, tongue, lips and naso-pharynx form the vowels, but have absolutely no part in the production of the fundamental sound.

How, exactly, is this larynx, or nozzle, to be manipulated? Well, that is a controversial subject, since many teachers consider it anathema to even mention that "unmentionable" organ in polite company. Nevertheless, I am going to be tasteless enough to dare to open the subject.

Let me first go on record as saying that many fine vocalists have been effectively trained to perform without ever having been made aware they even had a larynx. For them the throat is only an open pipe through which the air passes and one is not supposed to feel any sensation in it when singing. I am not about to criticize this concept since I was personally trained in that manner for twenty-five years by my third teacher, Samuel Margolis. It worked well enough for me at that time, so why complain?

But while many fine vocalists advocate an approach that religiously avoids any reference to the larynx, there are many who disagree. The first time I ever thought about having a larynx was when I did an interview for *Great Singers on Great Singing* with Bonaldo Giaiotti (mind you, I had been singing "larynxless" for almost forty years). I asked Bonaldo what an "open throat" meant to him and he replied that it was simply a lowered larynx, which he quickly demonstrated by dropping his Adam's/Eve's Apple and singing an Italian "ah" (the same rounded vowel used in the English word "awe"). I went home and shared this vocal tidbit with my Italian bride, Lucia, who suggested:

"Well, try seenging the 'ah' vowel that way." When I did, she observed, "That ees thee 'awe' vowel Margolis has been trying to get you to seeng for thee last twenty-five years."

I was astonished and my first thought was, "Why didn't Margolis simply tell me to lower my larynx, as Giaiotti did?" It was so simple! I could have saved twenty-five years of confusion on the subject! But, lest we forget, the larynx is supposed to be unmentionable, isn't it? Well, not anymore for me! Let us put an end right now to this sort of vocal censorship!

Further investigation on my part unearthed the fact that almost every successful singer in the business employed and advocated a lowered larynx. How does one go about this "lowering of the Adam's/Eve's Apple?" It is simple. Close your mouth and sniff briskly. You can easily feel with your fingers that the larynx goes down with each sniff. And that is nature's way of opening the throat. Now this is not an internal function of the larynx itself. But this lowering is a change in laryngeal position of great importance because you cannot—I repeat—cannot produce pure Italian vowels without it.

Lowering of the larynx is often mistakenly described as the "yawning position." But, watch it! There is no single "yawning position." A yawn is composed of a series of positions, the last of which would be a disaster for singing: it consists of a widely spread naso-pharynx, a distinctly closed throat, which can only produce strangled sounds.

Now, there are some very successful singers who steadfastly maintain they don't believe in "placement." This claim is commonly shrugged off by the skeptics who insist that such singers just had natural "placements" from the beginning and never had to seriously think about it. But, that is not necessarily true.

"Laryngeal singers" approach singing with the premise that the voice is produced by the larynx and they make no attempt to place it in the "mask." With such an approach, there is a slight sensation of "pinch" in the larynx. This can be regarded as a form of "chest voice" since there is no sensation of placement above the vocal folds when employing it. Bear in mind that this refers to the male chest voice, which is the same as the female's "belting" voice. Such an approach, commonly associated with the Melocchi School of singing, produces a bright, narrow and penetrating sound.

Producing an unmodified "ee-vowel" throughout the entire voice, without any placement in the mask is a form of pure chest voice, or "first-voice." From here on, we will refer to this form of chest voice as the "unmodified ee-track."

There is a corresponding modification of the first-voice based upon the "oo-vowel" which is achieved by going from the unmodified "ee" to "oo" by slightly shifting the back of the tongue to a lower position. The result is a very narrow "oo" felt as though it were being produced under the tongue, just behind the front of the chin. We will call this the "unmodified oo-track."

Unmodified vowels such as "oh" and "ah" are produced from the unmodified "oo" by simply opening the jaw wider. Likewise, the unmodified "ey" and "eh" vowels are also produced from the unmodified "ee" by opening the jaw wider.

Each of these unmodified vowels is a form of first-voice no matter where in the range they are to be found.

Another interesting form of chest voice is based upon a crooning sound, which the Italians call the "suono abbandonato," or "abandoned sound." By increased support, this sound can be enlarged to a full, powerful tone. Since this kind of sound is not placed in the mask, it is also a form of chest voice.

There is yet another function of the larynx, which is the antithesis of the "ee-track." It involves a pulling on, or stretching of the vocal folds, which produces what is commonly called "falsetto." We will refer to this sensation as the "shoehorn effect." (More about that in Chapter VIII.)

Teachers who advocate some sort of "placement" feel that directing attention to the larynx is anathema and they maintain that the throat should always feel like an empty pipe. In contrast, teachers who advocate the laryngeal approach say that since the sinusoidal resonating chambers cannot in any way be manipulated, the whole concept of placement is ridiculous.

This latter argument, however, does not really hold water since "placement" does not require any change in the shape of the sinusoidal resonators, but does require distinct changes in positions of the jaw, tongue, larynx, naso-pharynx and the soft palate which determine the paths the sound waves take.

If one approaches the subject with an open mind, it is obvious that either of these approaches is viable. There is plenty of evidence to back this up in the plethora of great soloists who have approached singing from either of these two schools. Let us keep an open mind and go on to the next chapter.

CHAPTER VI

PLACEMENT AND REGISTERS

In any study of vocal technique, "placement" is one of the most difficult subjects to tackle. There are radically different views as to where and how the voice should be placed and, as we have already noted in the previous chapter, there are very successful singers who maintain they don't believe in any "placement" at all.

Tied in with this is the even more touchy subject of "vocal registers." Asserting that they even exist evokes a cry of anguish from some teachers, but it is hard to defend their point of view if one seriously considers the obvious problems encountered by most male and female singers as they traverse the range between middle C and the first G above it. That there is a major problem—or change of register—in this span is hard to deny and we must not try to solve it by burying our heads in the sand and pretending it does not exist.

Women with light soprano voices often circumvent this problem by not using their so-called chest voice at all, thus avoiding the most problematic register change for both male and female voices. However, dramatic sopranos, mezzo sopranos and all male singers must meet this challenge. If, for example, the male does not master this register change, he will never acquire the complete two octave range required for singing opera.

Also consider what happens to most male singers when they imitate a female opera singer's high voice with a supported falsetto and then try to bring that full, bright sound down into their normal range without a break. It can be done by some, but most men find it difficult.

Jussi Bjoerling once told me that he did not have a falsetto. When I mentioned this to Dr. Leo Reckford, who treated us both, he said, "Of course he has a falsetto. It's just that he slips in and out of it so easily that he is not aware that anything is happening. All tenors should be able to make a smooth transition from falsetto to chest voice. Some baritones are also able to do it, but no basses."

I took the bit about "no basses" as a personal challenge and eventually found the secret of how to do it, a matter which we will discuss in Chapter XI. The point I wish to make here is that there is more than enough evidence to show that all voices, male and female alike, have three register changes.

One register change may not be as obvious as another and is sometimes only perceived as a slight alteration of texture in the sound or, in extreme cases, by pitch problems or weakness in some specific part of the voice.

Those who accept the existence of registers generally agree that there are four. Adopting this premise, we will call these registers "the four voices." Despite this proposed fragmentation of the voice into four components, our goal must eventually be to make all four sound as though they were one.

Using the notation from the Harvard Dictionary of Music (1986) we will denote middle C by c'; the first C below it by c, the second

C below that by C; and the first C above middle C by c''; the second C above it by c'''; etc.; let us consider the registers and the "pivot notes" between them for the common voice categories:

	low note		1st pivot		2nd pivot		high note		whistle tones
Coloratura soprano:	a#	<->	f#'	<->	e''	<->	d'''	<->	f''
Lyric soprano:	a#	<->	f#'	<->	e''	<->	c'''		
Dramatic soprano:	g#	<->	f'	<->	d#''	<->	c'''		
Mezzo soprano:	f#	<->	d#'	<->	c#''	<->	a#''		
Dramatic tenor:	B	<->	c#	<->	f#	<->	b'		
Lyric tenor:	c	<->	d'	<->	g'	<->	c''		
Baritone:	G#	<->	b	<->	e'	<->	g#'		
Bass-baritone:	G	<->	a#	<->	d#'	<->	g'		
Bass:	F	<->	a	<->	d'	<->	f'		

The male singer basically employs his lower three voices; his fourth and highest voice is not used on the stage except for comic effect or unless he is a countertenor. Women have the same low first-voice as men do, but they do not call it chest voice: it is the sound they use in popular music for "belting," sometimes referred to as "raw chest." When singing opera they seldom, if ever, use this voice, basically employing only the upper three.

What women commonly call "chest voice" is actually the male's "second" or "middle voice." Then comes the major transition just above middle C into what we will call the "third-voice." Women usually call that the "middle voice" and it is the male's "high voice." There is yet one transition above this into the "supported falsetto," which is the legitimate "high voice" for the woman. We will call this the "fourth-voice."

Four schools of singing have sprung up around the isolation and employment of these registers or "voices." Teachers usually concentrate on the basic sound that is associated with one particular voice and then try to make their students carry that sound throughout their entire range with no perceptible change in register. This yields at least four different, but viable approaches to singing.

One teacher wants the voice placed "up and over—behind the eyeballs," while another wants the voice to be placed "down in the larynx—beneath the back of the tongue." Another wants the voice suspended in the dome of the hard palate—with "a mouthful of sound," and then there is the one that wants the voice placed absolutely "nowhere."

Each of these approaches employs different muscle complexes in and around the larynx, tongue, naso-pharynx and soft palate, which can be called into action to produce sounds in different ways. I, personally, have been able to isolate and employ all four approaches, and when one certain vocal approach is not functioning correctly, I specifically concentrate on it in my vocal exercises until it is fully restored. I then coordinate all these approaches together so they sound like only one.

Let us begin by discussing the three basic schools of singing that do employ "placement," after which we can consider the laryngeal school, which does not.

"Placement" is commonly associated with very real feelings of vibration in different parts of the chest, throat and head, particularly in what is referred to as the "mask" or "maschera" as it is called in Italian.

Most women describe the mask as that region around and behind the eyeballs including the sinuses and the nasal passages. Some men include the dome of the hard palate and the upper teeth when speaking of the mask.

Manipulations of the jaw, tongue, larynx, soft palate and naso-pharynx produce corresponding sensations of vibration in various locations in the throat, head and chest. This cause and effect relationship enables us to focus our attention on these different locations at will.

The sinuses, which constitute a major part of the mask, are considered by many singers and pedagogues to be important resonators for producing the bigger-than-life sound needed for singing opera. This is probably false. Experiments were conducted in which a subject's sinuses were filled with water and then sealed off with wax after which the subject was made to sing. Sealing off the sinuses purportedly caused no distinguishable change in the sound, which would indicate that the main resonators are actually the mouth, the naso-pharynx, the pharynx and the larynx.

Does there seem to be one correct placement for all voices? The answer often given is "no," with the logical argument that we are all constructed differently: some people have broad faces and others narrow ones; some have cavernous throats and some are barrel-chested, etc. Obviously, resonance chambers come in a variety of shapes and sizes and a singer must find his/her natural place of maximum resonance under the guidance of a competent teacher.

But there is an added complication: as we have already stated in the Introduction, there are differences other than the ones just named. Although both men and women have essentially the same basic naso-pharyngeal and laryngeal physiology, there is the quantitative difference of size to be taken into account. The basic construction of a violin is essentially the same as that of a cello, but due to their difference in size, they cannot possibly be played in the same manner. When playing the cello, you certainly cannot put it under your chin as you would a violin. Yet the basic construction of both instruments is the same, the real difference being that of size.

The same logic holds true for all human voices, both male and female. Here the major difference is that of size of the vocal folds. So, qualitative differences in shape, as well as quantitative differences in size, will determine how individual voices are best to be "placed."

But we must be aware of the simple fact that a singer can also employ variations in "placement" to adapt to differences in the range in which one sings. That, of course, brings us back to the subject of registers. It is natural to want to smooth the path between registers, because nothing sounds worse than the singer who very clearly shifts gears in going from one register to another.

51

I know that Maria Callas is revered as one of the greatest opera singers of all time. But I clearly remember the criticism that was constantly leveled at her when she was in full career: she sounded as though she were singing with three different voices. People today tend to forget this, but it was very real—and certainly a drawback.

There is one vital problem that is often ignored: many teachers and singers think there is only one correct way to place the voice, but since different frequencies of sound require different size resonance chambers for maximum results, one can easily fall into a serious trap. When a teacher tells a male student with a strong middle voice to "bring it up into the high range without any change in placement," he may succeed in doing just that, but will have to work a little harder than necessary in the upper range. Or, vice versa, when a male student with naturally heroic high notes is instructed to "bring the sound down to the middle without any change in placement," he will most likely end up with a muddy middle voice.

I was fundamentally trained to sing with the "second-voice," being taught to imagine that my vocal folds were located in the dome of the hard palate. I was told to think of starting the tone from above—to assure that I was "singing on the breath" instead of "with the breath." It produced a sensation of drawing the sound out of the throat into the mouth, instead of pushing it up from below. It feels like having a mouthful of sound. This is commonly accompanied by a slight protrusion of the lips, especially in the high voice.

For twenty-five years I unquestioningly followed this approach, under the tutelage of Samuel Margolis, the only teacher of Robert Merrill. Singing in this manner worked well enough for Bob and me over a period of many, many years. Listen to Merrill's magnificent sound and try to say this approach was not viable. I had the same basically rich sound produced in part by this technique and in part by natural endowment.

Bob and I were especially comfortable in the middle voice and were certainly able to make a good sound in the upper voice as well. However, there were other male singers who did not have such great middle voices, but had the most extraordinary high notes. Leonard Warren, for example, could not quite match the rich middle voice of Merrill, yet no one could match Leonard's thrilling high notes.

Did Warren just have a freak instrument? I don't believe so. True, he had a God-given instrument, but he also had a very different approach to placement which favored his high voice and muddied up the middle a bit. While Merrill and I were being taught to place the voice in the dome of the hard palate, Warren's teacher probably advocated a placement that was deep in the throat, behind and under the back of the tongue. I assure you that as I kept the placement of my high notes in the dome of the hard palate, I made a decent sound, but it was axiomatic to me that one had to work harder in the upper register than in the middle and lower.

I became curious about those special male singers who had incredible high voices from day one and yet had an opaque sound in the middle. I was bewildered, even skeptical, when they claimed that their high notes were as easy as middle voice, if not easier. But they demonstrated the truth of what they said by having beautiful pianissimi in the upper register as well.

It was not until I began to experiment with shifting the placement of my high notes to a position deep behind and beneath the back of my tongue that my high voice began to feel as easy as my middle voice. This approach is sometimes accompanied by cocking the head back in the high voice. One singer with great high notes that resorted to this was Eugene Conley. As he approached each high note, he cocked his head back, drawing it down toward his shoulders.

A third school of singing involves raising the soft palate and feeling the main resonance behind the eyeballs. It is often described as thinking "back, up and over." This striving for resonance—high in the head, above and behind the hard palate—tends to make the male voice quite clear and easy to handle, but somewhat thinned out in quality. Even though such a sound is purported to "carry" in the theater, it does not usually produce the more generous sound of the true Verdi-type heavyweights.

However, for the high voice of the female singer this approach is optimal. If you are a male singer, you can test this by singing with a clear ringing falsetto so it sounds like a female opera singer. You will find the optimum sound for supported, high falsetto is achieved by placing the sound up behind the eyeballs. This approach is often accompanied by the external sign of raising the eyebrows on high notes.

The approach we have yet to discuss is the one in which, purportedly, there is no placement at all.

When male and female singers alike have reached the highest notes possible in the upper voice, a switch to the very forward, pinched production, called "falsettone" in Italian, will allow them to go at least half an octave higher. It will prove to be interesting and controversial to explore the idea that the "falsettone" is a high extension of the unmodified "ee- and oo-tracks," which are a form of chest voice. Does this imply that the very high notes, called "whistle tones," used by the coloratura singing the Queen of the Night are to be considered chest voice? More of that in the next chapter.

Now, of the four schools that have grown out of the four basic resonance chambers, one school might initially be somewhat better for a singer with a certain physiognomy and another might prove to be better for someone else. Since you have to start somewhere, it is best to begin training with the school that seems to work best for you. But, consider this challenging thought: you should eventually learn to employ all four of these schools, since each of them could be important for a different, specific part of your range.

In considering the idea of four distinct "voices," recall the cliche/axiom of imagining a ball floating on top of a fountain. This raises a practical question that usually remains unanswered simply because it is not asked. Where is this ball supposed to be located? The answer to this will vary according to which of the four voices one is employing at the moment. But more of that as we proceed.

There is one basic thought that should be constantly kept in mind: all the vowel sounds produced should be the pure and undistorted

Italian vowels. If the placement you are using does not produce these pure, undistorted vowels, then it is not right for you.

We have not yet touched upon what is often called the Melocchi School, one that employs no placement at all. But this is a chapter on "placement," is it not? So, it has no place here. Patience; we will examine this approach in-depth when discussing the first-voice.

CHAPTER VII

THE FIRST-VOICE

The "first-voice" is what men call "chest" and women refer to as "belting" or "raw chest"—not to be confused with what women call "chest" and which men refer to, as their "middle voice." Since male opera singers basically use their three lower voices and female opera singers use their three upper voices, this chapter on the first-voice might superficially appear to be of greater interest to men than to women. However, there will be some unexpected insights for the female singer, so I urge you ladies to take this chapter seriously. And, surprisingly, you will find that I acquired some of my deepest understanding of the first-voice from two coloratura sopranos, Patrice Munsel and Rita Shane.

In this book we shall consider four widely practiced approaches to voice training, each of which is based upon the development of but one of the four "voices." This chapter will be devoted to different aspects of training the first-voice.

But let me warn you, if you are serious about exploring new vocal concepts, remember that while it is always good to add something new to your technique, it should never be done at the cost of losing what has served you well in the past. Do not think for a moment that embracing new ideas means your original approach was wrong, particularly if you have already successfully reached a professional level of performing. As you add new ideas, constantly return to the things you were always able to do and make sure they still work for you.

When I began studying voice with Gennaro Curci in 1937, he said, "The low voice is your foundation. When that goes, it is the end."

As the years passed, I saw his prediction fulfilled time and time again with older singers who could still produce brilliant high notes, but who had ended up with thin or foggy low and middle voices and who had to take twice as many breaths as they should to finish a phrase. These symptoms always foreshadowed the end of their careers and have generally been accepted as the inevitable consequences of aging.

Physiologically, these problems arise from a "bowing" of the vocal folds, said to be due to a weakening of the laryngeal muscles with age. This bowing allows an increasing quantity of air to escape during phonation, resulting in the fogginess and shortness of breath just described.

When I reached my middle sixties, I too found my low and middle range thinning out. My first reaction was to accept it as the beginning of the end. But then I decided to tackle it purely as a problem in technique—and it turned out to be just that!

When youngsters begin studying voice, they usually have natural low and middle voices, but poor high notes. And no matter what one says, it is a fact of life that the public wants great high notes from all singers—including basses. So the quest for high notes starts early and never ends!

How often young singers are told that the reason they have no high notes is that they are singing too fat and heavy in the middle.

With this thought in mind, many mature singers begin to avoid a full "chest" sound as though it were detrimental to the voice and they even brag about having learned to sing on the "interest" instead of the "capital" (Have you not noticed that most of your friends who "live on the interest" have retired?). These mature artists assure us that they have finally learned how to "sing easily"— and you can be sure of one thing—they are "easing" themselves right out of a career.

As I turned seventy-four, I was examined by a prominent voice therapist who was amazed that my vocal folds showed no sign of the bowing one would expect in a singer of my age. Although this bowing is generally accepted as an irreversible consequence of laryngeal muscles weakening in the so-called Golden Years, there is a very good reason for the unusual strength of my vocal folds which tends to discredit this opinion.

So what is the secret of how I manage to continue singing as I do in my mid-seventies? Well, there are many reasons, but one of the most important is that I still spend the "capital" when I perform— and this "capital" is principally to be found in the first-voice.

The Fundamental-First-Voice or "Abbandonato"

The "fundamental-first-voice" is what women call "belting" and it was Patrice Munsel who made me realize that it is related to the "belly laugh." Try a belly laugh with its deep exhalations of breath, accompanied by a rumbling vibration under the sternum. These deep exhalations keep the production of the sound completely relaxed and free of laryngeal gripping.

Another way to find this deep chest sound is to visit a farm and listen to the lowing of the cows. If you accurately imitate their mooing, you will essentially produce the same sound as the belly laugh (be very sure there are no bulls around when you try it). This is what we shall call the "fundamental-first-voice" and it produces no sensation of placement in the mask, being basically felt under the sternum. This is the most relaxed, abandoned sound one can make. When properly produced, there is a sensation of a second "appoggio" on, or below the vocal folds with the breath being blown upwards through them.

It is possible to carry this fundamental-first-voice up through the male singer's entire range. Although I do not recommend this as a basic approach for singing, it will be of value to explore how it can be done. For the fundamental-first-voice to be carried up into the range associated with the second-voice, it must be based upon what the Italians call "abbandonato," a sound I associate with the "crooning" of Bing Crosby (forgive me if I show my age by referring to "The Groaner," but the way he sang was what crooning was all about). This crooning sound is accomplished by relaxing the vocal folds and just blowing the air through.

If you can't find any old Bing Crosby records, then listen to those of Ezio Pinza. When he sings mezza-voce, you will hear a warm, crooning sound produced with a large spacing in the throat (without any lateral spreading of the naso-pharynx, of course). Believe me, his crooning mezza-voce was not lost over the foot-lights, it literally filled the theatre with sound. I know, because I, as a young singer, often heard it and strove to imitate it.

I soon discovered that when this sound is intensified by increased support it can be turned into a large, impressive forte. As an extension of the fundamental-first-voice, this sound is produced without placement in the mask.

With practice, the male singer can also take this more abandoned sound all the way up through the range associated with his "third-voice." However to accomplish this, in approaching the range of the "third-voice," one must lower the larynx and employ the sensation commonly referred to as the "gagging position," or the "shoehorn sensation," which is felt down under the back of the tongue.

Male singers with dramatic voices often describe the accompanying sensation as "feeling like a second appoggio" in the region of the vocal folds.

Carrying the first-voice up into the higher range produces a slightly darker sound than usual, but it can be impressive in size. It is basically a safe sound to make since it provides a cushion of air between the vocal folds and protects them from abrasion. In fact, this is the one sort of sound you can safely make using the *full power* of your support without any control from diaphragmatic appoggio.

I have used it with great effect in *Don Carlo* when singing "presso il Grande Inquisitor" in the third act duet with Philip. The Inquisitor's potentially deadly phrase, ascending stepwise up to the high F, has been the nemesis of many a bass, but becomes much easier to produce when using this approach.

It is a completely different story with the merciless high F two pages earlier. After a tremendous outburst, all in the most difficult passaggio of the bass voice (D-natural above middle C), the Inquisitor has to sing "tranquilli lascio andar..." with the "ee" vowel on the high F. Here I revert to a deep unmodified "ee" with plenty of "smile under the sternum." The important fact is that these phrases which used to be so terribly difficult for me as a young singer are no longer a problem.

As we continue to study the first-voice, we will find that the fundamental-first-voice is but one of the possible modifications of true "chest." These modifications can be achieved in different ways through certain manipulations of, and by, the larynx. Let us now discuss another important modification of the fundamental-first-voice which we will call the "unmodified ee-track."

The "Unmodified Ee-Track"

Surprisingly, the solution to my low voice dilemma did not come from working on the low voice, but on the high. For many years I had noticed that if I began a lesson with weak low notes, they definitely improved after vocalizing in the upper register. I had been aware of this phenomena for a long time, but had no idea as to why it was so.

In my later years of vocal experimentation, I worked on producing an unmodified "ee" vowel throughout my high range and, without question, it definitely restored the strength of my low and middle voices.

But first, we must clarify what is meant by an *unmodified* "ee" vowel. The *unmodified* "ee" vowel must be produced throughout the entire voice without any sensation of placement in the mask or mouth. It will be a sound that obviously originates in the larynx, and a sound that can be modified by a sensation of smiling under the sternum.

When you employ this "unmodified ee-track" correctly there is absolutely no sensation of placement above the vocal folds throughout your entire range. And when you start a sound using the unmodified ee-track you will have the sensation of closing the vocal folds before engaging the breath. In the larynx, it will feel as though you were picking up the note as you would pick up a pencil from the table with your thumb and first finger—and this is true no matter how high the pitch. You should develop a controlled strength in the larynx which will enable you to cleanly pick the highest notes in your range out of the air without a harsh attack. But remember, this is only possible when you maintain a very strong sensation of compression, with your Support/Appoggio keeping the breath pressure away from your vocal folds.

Once you can produce the unmodified "ee" vowel, it is very simple to go to the unmodified "ey" and "eh" vowels. As we have already noted in Chapter IV, all one has to do is slowly open the jaw and "ee" first becomes "ey" and then "eh." Going to the unmodified "ah" vowel is a bit trickier.

The "Unmodified Oo-Track"

It is easier to go from the unmodified "ee" to an unmodified "oo" rather than an unmodified "ah" because "oo" is made with the same closed position of the jaw as "ee." But it is essential to remember: NO LIPS for the unmodified "oo" vowel; it is produced deep in the throat, as is the unmodified "ee." The main difference between the unmodified "ee" and the unmodified "oo" should be a slight flattening of the rear of the tongue, with absolutely no change in the position of the jaw.

Corresponding to the "unmodified ee-track," there is an "unmodified oo-track" which encompasses the entire range of the voice. It might be easier for the male singer to find the deep sensation associated with the proper production of the unmodified "oo" vowel by starting a high note with an "n", singing "noo". For the female singer this should be done in what she calls her "middle voice." In producing this unmodified "oo," there should be no accompanying sensation of placement above the vocal folds.

The unmodified "oo" vowel has a slight tightening sensation felt just under the tongue, which is similar to the pinch associated with the unmodified "ee" vowel.

Now try going from the unmodified "oo" to the unmodified "oh" and the unmodified "ah" by just opening the jaw a bit wider and you will have all the vowels in an unmodified form.

When I first succeeded in producing unmodified vowels throughout my entire range, they were definitely not of the quality I would care to use on the stage. I realized that I would have to modify this approach for two major reasons: a) the sound had to be more pleasing and b) the pinched tightness necessary to produce the sound could be dangerous and had to be relieved.

As I searched for modifications of the pure unmodified vowels that would be more viable for public performance, I began enriching them by the sensation of "smiling under the sternum," which I mentioned earlier. The space where I felt the resonance was now located below the larynx, not above it, with the sound seeming to come from under the sternum or from the chest.

The difference between this and the "fundamental-first-voice" lies in adding the sensation of the "pinch-effect" in the larynx.

WARNING! Do not allow the sensation of smiling under the sternum to reach up above your vocal folds. This leads to a spreading of the naso-pharynx, which is undesirable!

Enrico Caruso once told Rosa Ponselle to "keep a square throat" (see *Great Singers on Great Singing*—the chapter on Rosa Ponselle). The meaning of that statement eluded me for years but, if I am now guessing right, the base of Caruso's "square throat" was seated under the sternum and was based on the first-voice. Ponselle felt this advice was of great value to her, so perhaps other female singers should be encouraged to try it.

I found that if I kept this "smile under the sternum" as I went down the scale, my middle and low voice both remained consistently strong. However, relaxing the "pinch-effect" and reverting to the relaxed sensation of the fundamental- first-voice can produce an even richer sound.

Diligently practicing the "pinch-effect" through both the unmodified "ee" and "oo" vowels led me to a vocal rejuvenation and effectively reversed the condition of "bowing" that was affecting my vocal folds. It also gave me some insight into what is meant by "chest voice," or at least one form of it.

The late Dr. Leo Reckford once said to me, "Extend your first two fingers and pretend they are your vocal cords." He then tugged on them, saying, "That's *falsetto*." Then he squeezed my fingers together at the knuckles and said, "That's chest." According to what we have just discussed, it is, at least, a modification of the chest voice, or "first-voice," as we have agreed to call it.

This kind of first-voice is not a phenomenon restricted to the low range, but can be employed throughout one's entire range, which would normally include all four voices. And there are quite a few singers who have had long careers singing with their first-voice alone.

If you carry this particular form of first-voice all the way throughout your entire range, you will discover that there is absolutely no register change. Of course, this would lend support to the claims of some teachers that there are no register changes in the voice. But that would be like driving your car from New York to California in first gear and then claiming that the car only had one gear. Actually, the truth would be that you did not have a proper understanding of your car's design.

Since practicing with this modification of the first-voice resolved my problem in the low and middle ranges, my problem proved to be a technical one and not the result of aging. This showed once and for all that such a condition is reversible.

Now let us discuss the pros and cons of employing this approach of unmodified vowels throughout one's entire voice as a basic technique. First, consider the dangers of using the pinch-effect. Most singers who say they do not believe in placement basically use this kind of first-voice throughout their entire vocal range. Some people mistakenly assume they are just blessed with a natural placement. The fact is they are literally *not using any placement at all.*

For example, when singers make facial grimaces when singing, it is usually indicative of what they are trying to accomplish internally, and the only facial grimace that the great Luciano Pavarotti employs is a pulling down of the corners of his mouth. Most likely, this is an external sign of attempting some sort of "spacing" below the larynx, which I have already described as "smiling under the sternum." In my interview with him in *Great Singers on Great Singing,* he firmly maintained he did not place his voice in the "maschera."

Now, this sort of laryngeal approach to singing is often referred to as the "Melocchi School." Melocchi was the teacher of Mario Del Monaco and it is said that he espoused producing the voice exclusively in the larynx without any form of placement.

I had occasion to perform the role of Ramphis in *Aida* with Mario Del Monaco when he did his first Radames at the Met and I must say that seldom in my life have I heard such a heroic sound come from a human throat. But what does making such a sound cost a singer in the long run?

One day, as I entered Dr. Reckford's office for a treatment, he greeted me with, "You know who just left? Del Monaco! When he sings he shouts, he forces, he yells...and I LIKE IT!"

He observed that Del Monaco's vocal cords were distinctly battered after every performance and that Mario, before leaving, had asked him whether or not he should change his technique. Reckford's answer was:

"So you damage your voice every time you sing. Let's face it, nobody sings forever—you included. If you change your technique you simply won't be Mario Del Monaco any more. No, keep on singing exactly the way you do. Don't change a thing."

Bear in mind that the Melocchi approach can be risky to employ. The first time I personally experimented with it was right after my interview with Luciano Pavarotti for *Great Singers on Great Singing* in which he espoused a laryngeal way of singing. Although Luciano does not produce the gigantic sound of Mario Del Monaco, his approach is similar to that espoused by Melocchi. Obviously, Luciano does not use the devastating pressure of breath that Del Monaco did and he does not damage his voice when he sings, making him living proof that the laryngeal approach can be quite feasible when used properly.

I later discussed the Melocchi method with Franco Corelli, knowing he had been influenced by it in his early years. He maintained that the approach was "valid, but had to be used with great moderation." The problem is what did Corelli mean by "moderation"?

When I initially experimented with starting the sound in the larynx, I quickly got hoarse. Nevertheless, I refused to give up and continued trying it a little at a time. Within a few weeks I was no longer getting hoarse and realized the problem I had experienced was due to weak laryngeal muscles going into a fatigued spasm and was not due to actual damage to the delicate vocal folds.

When I sang this way my vocal production seemed a bit tight, but there was a positive side to it as well: for the first time in my life my tongue lay relaxed and forward, touching the back of my lower teeth. I had previously tended to pull my tongue back when singing, which somewhat distorted the vowels. My wife, Lucia, commented on how pure the vowel sounds were when I sang this way, but she also noted that my voice sounded distinctly narrower and a bit more baritonal in quality.

I then tried to sing a performance of Mephistopheles in *Faust* using this laryngeal approach. The result? Halfway through the show I was so vocally fatigued that I was forced to abandon this method to finish the opera. Luckily, I had my old technique to fall back on. This impelled me to give more thought to Corelli's admonition to use this method with "great moderation." I was attracted by its positive results, yet intimidated by its potential problems.

Years ago, I was of the opinion that singers with very brilliant, trumpet-like voices tended to fold up vocally in their earlier years, whereas those with darker, warmer voices tended to last longer. But was that impression really true? Take a look at the record.

Remember that Mario Del Monaco was still singing at the age of sixty, and consider other famous singers of the past who successfully employed a laryngeal approach. Certainly, Enrico Caruso sang that way, but it is well known that he had nodes removed surgically more than once. That is a poor recommendation.

Richard Tucker also employed a laryngeal approach and back in 1946 his technique seemed a bit tight to some of my colleagues, who predicted he would not be singing in five years. Time and Richard certainly proved them wrong and, for my money, he was the greatest American tenor of them all. Yes, he outlived his critics and when he died in his 60's, he was still singing better than any of the youngsters. So Richard is a very positive recommendation for this method.

And then there was Lauritz Melchior. When I first sang with him, his vocal production reminded me of "squeezing toothpaste out of a toothpaste tube." But what a heroic sound that man made, a sound that literally shook the walls of the theater. I often wondered how a human throat could stand such forceful treatment? Yet consider that his career with the Metropolitan was brought to an untimely end at the age of sixty-seven, when "Der Bingle" fired him for insubordination. Since that time I have never heard another Helden-tenor that I would consider his worthy successor.

I have also marvelled how Giovanni Martinelli managed to maintain such a squeezed but powerful sound in dramatic reper-toire over so many years. Yet the last time I heard him in person was at the Hollywood Bowl where he successfully sang Canio in I Pagliacci at the age of sixty-eight.

If you also include Pavarotti in this list, the pluses certainly outnumber the minuses.

This technique can definitely be used throughout your entire vocal range and to good effect, but it is probably the most difficult and risky of the four basic approaches since it requires a much more critical dependence upon Support/Appoggio, without which one could easily slip into dangerous glottal attacks and strong abrasion between the vocal folds.

To avoid these problems in actual performance, I recommend modifying each attack with a slight impulse of breath, almost a half-h, instead of employing the more risky approach of "picking up the tone." This little modification makes the attack safer and begins providing an important cushion of air.

An interesting facet of the first-voice is the "falsettone," a sound that can be produced by both by men and women alike. The falsettone is a pinched, brilliant sound that is found in and above the range of the fourth-voice. But it is not actually part of the fourth-voice, being an extension of the first-voice or "chest," carried up extremely high into the range generally associated with the woman's high voice or fourth-voice.

What men call falsettone, women call "whistle tones." The Met coloratura, Rita Shane was the one that introduced me to it by producing a high piercing glissando that went well above the soprano's normal range. Now, here is the real surprise: this use of whistle tones, or falsettone, by which coloratura sopranos reach their stratospheric high F's in the Queen of the Night's treacherous second aria, are nothing more than a modification of chest, or first-voice. And this is also used by most bel-canto tenors to reach their high D-naturals.

When a male singer produces a completely unmodified "ee" vowel in his high range, its continuation up into the range of the high falsetto is that same "falsettone," or "whistle- tone" and, as we have already noted, it is nothing more than one particular modification of pure "chest." This kind of sound is produced in a completely laryngeal manner with absolutely no placement in the mask.

Men, try a little experiment. Imitate the sound of a female opera singer above your normal singing range. This is a supported falsetto and not to be confused with the falsettone. You are now singing with your fourth-voice. Then take it as high in pitch as you can. Next, using the "laryngeal-pinch," put the sound more "forward" into a strong falsettone and you will find that you can now go half an octave higher than you could with just the supported falsetto. That is exactly what the coloratura soprano has to do to get those extreme high notes. Remember, it is nothing more than a form of pure chest.

When Rita Shane sang the "Queen of the Night," she produced just about the most powerful and impressive high F's I have ever heard. And I am thoroughly convinced that she was not just born with this ability, but that she developed it. I have already noted how she does a piercing glissando with the whistle tones or first-voice that runs well above the range of her fourth-voice. She says she begins doing this glissando the moment she gets up in the morning and continues doing it throughout the day. Again, this is nothing but pure chest, or first-voice.

It will be a good challenge for you singers, both male and female, to bring this high falsettone smoothly down to the lowest notes in your voice, using the "unmodified ee- track" all the way with no breaks or scratches. You can also do the same thing with the "oo-track." You may find it difficult at first, but it can be done. If I can do it, so can you!

If employing the "unmodified ee-track" is somewhat risky, why should we pursue it? I believe we should for the simple reason that when it is employed correctly, it will exercise and strengthen important laryngeal muscles of the chest voice without disturbing the rest of the voice as a whole. This will be of particular value to singers with dramatic voices, namely those who must sing extreme high notes and older professionals who are losing the middle and low. But, for heaven's sake, don't try it without a good teacher to guide you—that is—if you can find one who has the slightest inkling of what I am talking about.

Conclusion

It is easily seen that the "unmodified ee-track" favors the "ee"-"ey"-"eh" vowels, whereas the "unmodified oo-track" favors the "oo"-"oh"-"ah" vowels. So, a student who has been exercised by using the both the "unmodified ee-track" and the "unmodified oo-track" will generally be equally comfortable with all vowels in the high range, whether modified or not.

Whether one uses the fundamental-first-voice, the "unmodified ee-track," or the "unmodified oo-track," the result in each case is one of absolutely no sensation of placement of the voice above the vocal folds. These three approaches are all modifications of the first-voice.

Now is the proper moment to return to the cliché of the "ball floating on the fountain." As I stated before, the question, "Where is the ball supposed to be located?" usually goes unanswered simply because it is never asked. It is logical to imagine that for the first-voice the ball should be floating in the region of the sternum, just under the vocal folds, which, as we shall see, will *not* be the case with the other three voices.

I would like to conclude this chapter by mentioning another, even more important form of vocal modification which is effected by switching to either the second-, third- or fourth-voices in the appropriate ranges. As you can see, I do not advocate basing one's entire vocal approach on the first-voice, although it can be done. This shifting between the voices will alleviate the necessity of basing one's entire technique on just one voice.

CHAPTER VIII

THE SECOND-VOICE

The "second-voice" encompasses the male singer's middle range. The female singer calls it "chest," which is not to be confused with what the male singer calls "chest," or the first-voice. What will be said here concerning the approach to the male's second-voice will apply equally well to the woman's so-called chest voice.

As noted before, many successful schools of singing are based upon training one of the four voices. It is not surprising that particular students will tend to favor each particular approach. This is in accord with the opinion that there is not just one specific placement for all voices, since we are all built somewhat different physiologically.

The resonator that favors the second-voice is in the front of the mouth, extending up into the dome of the hard palate. I feel qualified to speak on that subject since I was trained in such an approach for twenty-five years by Samuel Margolis.

When I first went to Margolis I had a problem with the A-natural just under middle C. I was using a heavy chest sound below the A-natural and a brighter, baritonish sound above it, with a distinct shift of register. The trouble was localized at the passing note itself, where I had a crippling scratch in the voice when I tried to sing forte.

During a performance with Jussi Bjoerling of Il Trovatore on the Metropolitan Opera tour, I was in my dressing room hammering away at that troublesome break. Jussi abruptly threw open the door and said sharply:

"Stop that! You'll ruin your voice!" He left just as abruptly as he had entered, leaving me facing an open door, perplexed and not knowing what to do next. I wanted to explain that if I didn't batter my voice into submission, I wouldn't be able to sing in that problem range at all. From that frustration and confusion came my firm decision to study voice with Samuel Margolis upon my return to New York.

The Fundamental-Second-Voice

Margolis based his approach to placement on what we will call the "fundamental-second-voice," an approach he wanted carried both upwards and downwards throughout one's entire range. The imagery he used for this particular modification of the second-voice was to imagine the vocal cords to be located in the dome of the hard palate where the sound should begin, instead of in the throat.

A good parallel to this imagery for the fundamental-second-voice would be the cliché of singing with "pear-shaped tones," with the understanding that the "fat end of the pear" would be located up in the front of the mouth, filling the dome of the hard palate.

Margolis constantly spoke of "starting the tone from above, with the throat feeling like an empty pipe." This is similar to imagining having a "soap bubble full of sound in the mouth," or simply a "mouthful of sound." The idea of "starting the tone from above" can also be related to the popular cliché of "drinking the tone."

In the previous chapter we discussed the imagery of "a ball bouncing on the top of a fountain of water" and, for the first-voice, we imagined the ball to be hovering under the vocal folds. However, when employing the second-voice, the ball should be imagined floating in the dome of the hard palate, just behind the upper teeth. There must always be a delicate balance of breath pressure under the larynx so that one is not aware of the breath originating from below (even though it actually does). On the contrary, if one drives the breath up through the larynx from below, while trying to focus the sound in the mask, it can be most harmful. (The Italians call this singing "col fiato" instead of "sul fiato," or, "with the breath," instead of "on the breath.")

The "Unmodified-Second-Voice"

As an exercise, it is helpful to employ yet another form of second-voice which is similar to the unmodified "ee" in the first-voice. It involves making a very bright, and needle-pointed sound aimed directly at the region of the nostrils. There is a pinching sensation associated with this approach, just as there is with the "unmodified ee-track." The location of the pinch sensation is not in the region of the vocal folds, but in the region just under the front of the tongue, extending down to a point just behind the tip of the chin. I do not advocate using this rather gripped approach for singing but, like the "unmodified ee-track," when employed occasionally as a vocal developer, it has merit.

Note that just as the three modifications of the first-voice had one thing in common, namely that they were not associated with any sensation of placement in the maschera, so do the three modifications of the second-voice have one thing in common, namely that they are all placed and felt up in the front of the mouth.

Placement, Vocal Color & Vowels

Now that we are no longer dealing with the first-voice, we can freely pursue the subjects of "placement," "color of voice" and "vowel sounds."

I always found it interesting that each of Margolis' students came out of his studio sounding somewhat different from the other: they did not fit into some particular mold as did pupils of many other prominent teachers. This was because the Maestro did not have any preconceived preference for a certain color of voice.

Margolis maintained that if one sang with pure, undistorted Italian vowels, the resulting sound would be correctly produced and show one's natural and individual color. Now the only way you can know for sure that your vowels are pure and undistorted is to be under the guidance of a knowledgeable teacher. The hard part is to find a teacher who really knows the meaning and origin of the Italian adage "La lingua Toscana in bocca Romana" (the Tuscan language in the mouth of the Roman).

The Italian "ah", for example, is not the same "ah" you hear in the German or French languages. It is a deeper, more open-throated vowel pronounced as in the English word "awe", and such an open-throated vowel is only achieved by lowering the larynx and amply opening the jaw. In fact, all Italian vowels should be produced with a lowered larynx.

Since the Maestro had based his approach on the fundamental-second-voice, studying with him served to lighten up the heavy approach I had been using in my low and middle range. After working with him for three months, the break in my middle voice disappeared. The scratch on my A-natural was mastered by using the following scale:

Mee---------------Ah--------------------

Meh---------------Ah--------------------------

This scale was to be sung as briskly as possible, with a slight impulse between all the notes (Margolis described the impulse as a "half-h"), and everything went well with me except when I made the rapid turn in the neighborhood of my problematic A-natural. It was there that my scale became quite clumsy and I was forced to slow up considerably.

I was obviously making some sort of exaggerated muscular change in going from the A-flat to the B-flat. So my challenge was to find one common setting of the throat for singing both above and below that change of register, since an exaggerated muscular change could not be accommodated to the speed and agility required by this exercise.

Margolis pointed out that I was losing the impulse, or half-h, on the problem turn because of rigidity in my vocal production and that I needed a greater flexibility in order to master the scale in this range. He explained this meant that the "impulse," or half-h, which was required between all notes, had to come from the diaphragm, not the throat.

After three months of sweating over this particular exercise, I conquered it and the problem of the scratch left me for good. What solved my problem? It was simple—I employed a slight rotating sensation deep in my larynx where the vocal folds are located (a sensation which can be likened to a shoehorn being gently applied deep behind and under the tongue).

Applying this throat setting kept my larynx gently lowered as I ascended from the range of the first-voice to that of the second-voice and enabled me to smoothly bypass my problematic A-natural. I did not make any exaggerated shift in register because I was now singing almost exclusively in the second-voice. Although this approach solved a serious problem, it left me with a somewhat diminished lower range due to my abandonment of the first-voice. Unfortunately, the public makes special demands on the poor basso: he is not only supposed to have beautiful high notes, but rich low notes as well.

I suggested in the Introduction to this book that "every solution has its problems." Now you can see that in solving one of my problems, I had inadvertently acquired another in its place.

I have always admired the extraordinary voice of the great Spanish bass, José Mardones. He had the gorgeous high F of a basso cantante and yet his low and middle voice were like the rock of Gibraltar, with the sound of a true profundo. My voice had a dark, cavernous quality with easy high notes, but I could not figure out how Mardones produced that incredible profundo sound.

By nature, I was actually a true basso profundo—but a profundo stuck in "second gear." It was only after I began to study the development of the first-voice and its modifications that I was able to add a solid half octave to my low voice. But let's face it, despite my earlier limitation, I had many years of success based almost exclusively on the second-voice.

Margolis' approach, based upon fast moving coloratura type scales, was not intended to minimize the power of the sound. In fact, the Maestro always wanted to hear maximum volume together with maximum flexibility. And Bob Merrill and I certainly did not have small voices, even though we were trained to sing flexibly.

To see the picture clearer, we must realize that the difference between approaching the first-voice and the second-voice is a shift in imagining where the bouncing ball is located. This means that there is a definite change in technique when going from the first-voice to the second-voice.

When using the first-voice there is no placement in the mask at all, and in two of its three modifications one can be conscious of the involvement of the larynx, described by some as "a second appoggio" felt right on the vocal folds.

When one shifts exclusively to the fundamental-second-voice it definitely feels as though the voice were being produced in the dome of the hard palate and any pinch sensation, or second appoggio, associated with the first-voice is abandoned. The throat should then feel like an empty pipe.

Of course, it is advantageous to employ both the first and second-voices depending on the range involved. This advantage is best achieved by using the fundamental-first-voice in one's lowest range and then gently shifting to the fundamental-second-voice in the beginning of the next octave.

In such a shift, one must change the way the breath is employed. In the lower range of the fundamental-first-voice, the breath must be amply fed through the vocal folds from below, as in "crooning," with no sensation of placement in the maschera. When moving up into the fundamental-second- voice, one must shift to a sensation of drawing the air up into the dome of the soft palate, starting from above.

And when descending from the fundamental-second-voice to the first-voice, the opposite is true. In so doing, any sensation of placement in the mask must be abandoned and more air must be fed through the vocal folds.

Whereas shifting into the fundamental-second-voice in its appropriate range gives the voice a distinctly rich sound, remaining in a first-voice production with the pinch- effect in that range is viable, but the sound will be lighter and narrower and will require a bit more effort. It is analogous to failing to shift from first to second gear when driving your car on a long trip. You can still arrive at your destination, but not without risking damage to your car by constantly racing the motor.

I am completely convinced that when a woman sings in the range that she calls "chest," she should be very careful to place her voice in the dome of the hard palate, just as the male does in his middle voice. If she tries to keep the same placement in her so-called chest voice as she used in her middle voice, she will end up with a somewhat muddy sound.

CHAPTER IX

THE THIRD-VOICE

The "third-voice" is the male singer's "high voice" and the female singer's "middle voice." What will be said here will apply equally well to both male and female singers.

It used to be harder for me to sing in the high range (the third-voice) than in the middle (the second-voice), and every once in a while I was taken aback by some colleague who would claim the opposite. But it would disturb me even more when such a blessed one would have divine pianissimi in the high voice, while others, like I, did not.

My wife, Lucia, was one of those "fortunati" and it particularly irked me when she would say, "Darleeng, you have to be born weeth eet," since I have always disliked accepting any sort of limitation.

The "Fundamental-Third-Voice"

One of my baritone colleagues, Joseph Shore, who was blessed with extraordinary high notes, observed that men who were gifted as he was, often cocked their heads back when singing in the upper range (the third-voice). I previously spoke of Eugene Conley, the first American to ever sing an opening night at La Scala, and who always cocked his head back when singing high notes—and these were most impressive.

Realizing that external nuances are generally indicative of what a singer is trying to accomplish internally, I surmised that cocking the head back on high notes was intended to help place the sound in a space below the back of the tongue where the vocal folds are located.

A little experimentation showed me the validity of this approach and convinced me that I had found the proper placement for at least one modification of the third-voice, a modification which we will call the "fundamental-third-voice." Let me now describe how it differs from the fundamental-second-voice, even though they are related.

Consider again the cliché about singing with "pear-shaped" tones. I asked the question in Chapter I, "Where is the fat end of the pear located?" In the previous chapter on the second-voice, we decided it was up in the front of the mouth, filling the space that arches up into the dome of the hard palate. But in the fundamental-third-voice, the fat end is lodged down in the larynx where the vocal folds are located.

This is important enough to warrant using yet another kind of imagery. Imagine a long balloon and squeeze one end so that the other end bulges out. Imagine that the fat end is forward, filling the mouth when you use the fundamental-second-voice (a form of middle voice for the male and the so-called "chest voice" for the female). Then as you make the transition to the fundamental-third-voice (a form of high voice for the male and middle voice for the female), it is as though you have squeezed the front end and caused the back of the balloon to bulge out, a bulge that is felt down in the region behind the "Adam's/Eve's Apple."

To describe the complete sensation of spacing for resonance in the fundamental-third-voice, we now return to the image of using a shoehorn inserted in the larynx, down behind the tongue, and rotated back at the top and forward at the bottom (in the region of the vocal folds), much as you rotate a shoehorn to put a shoe on your foot.

Another way of describing the sensation in the throat when singing high notes properly is to think of what is commonly called the "gagging" position. What I am now about to describe may be to the point, or be completely off track. You be the judge:

One night in 1947, Angelo Casamassa, my dresser at the Old Met, came into my dressing room as I was leaning over the sink. He said, "That reminds me of Titta Ruffo. Every night, when I came into this very same dressing room, he was at the sink throwing up."

Ruffo is considered by many to be the greatest baritone of all time. Was he suffering from chronic nerves, or was he doing this on purpose to get the gagging sensation for his high notes? Well, sometimes singers will do some pretty strange things, so your guess is as good as mine. But I suspect the great Ruffo was seeking the gagging position.

The imagery of both the shoehorn and the gagging position accomplishes one simple thing—adding falsetto to the voice. Recall that in Chapter VII I mentioned how Dr. Leo P. Reckford had me extend the first two fingers of my hand, likening them to my vocal folds, and pulled on them saying, "That is falsetto." Then he squeezed my two fingers together at the second knuckles and said, "That is chest."

Well, that pulling on the vocal folds which adds falsetto to the voice is simply achieved by employing the shoehorn effect, or the gagging position.

As we have noted, the third-voice is the high range for the male singer and the middle range for the female singer. Its production and placement should be the same for both men and women. When attempting to completely isolate the fundamental-third-voice, there should be absolutely no sensation of placement in the front of the mouth. It should only be felt as a spacing in the throat, down under the back of the tongue, while the tone should feel as though it were going straight up from the vocal folds and out of the top of one's head.

As the male singer uses this lower, laryngeal space as the resonator for his fundamental-third-voice instead of any place in the frontal dome of the palate, the high notes should come more easily. An excellent test to see if you are doing this correctly is to sing the following scale all the way up through your highest range:

Mee----------------------Ah----------------

Meh--------------Ah--------------------

If singing this scale in your upper range does not feel as easy as singing in your middle voice, you probably are still resorting to the old habit of pulling the voice up front into the mask. To isolate the pure fundamental-third-voice with complete ease of singing in the upper range, one must abandon any frontal placement in the dome of the hard palate, yet maintain the shoehorn effect.

In this approach to the fundamental-third-voice, the ball bouncing on the fountain of water should now be pictured as floating just above the vocal folds, not under them as in the first-voice. The sound should seem to be starting from above—leaving the throat feeling like an empty pipe.

The shoehorn effect or gagging position, is antithetical to the "unmodified ee-track" described in the chapter on the first-voice. While the "unmodified ee-track" has a narrowed feeling in the throat, the shoehorn effect has the directly opposite feeling of spacing.

I recommend using the fundamental-tracks in professional singing. The unmodified "ee-" and "oo-tracks," when used in the upper range, are part and parcel of the laryngeal school of singing, which we have already seen to be quite viable.

I feel the unmodified "ee-" and "oo-tracks" are most valuable in strengthening the laryngeal muscles and should therefore be carefully, but fully developed. So let us continue our study of them in the third-voice.

The Unmodified "Ee" In The Third-Voice

As we noted in Chapter VII, the unmodified "ee" vowel can be carried all the way up through the entire range of the third-voice. As you ascend to the third-voice on this unmodified "ee" vowel, you must not open your jaw wider or spread your lips. Opening the jaw would modify the "ee" to "ih", while spreading the lips would encourage a lateral spreading of the naso-pharynx, which is anathema! A gentle pinching sensation will be experienced with taking the unmodified "ee" up into this range.

Of course, many voice teachers advocate modifying the vowel "ee" to "ih" in one's high voice by opening the jaw wider and abandoning the pinch sensation, letting the throat feel like an empty pipe. I have no quarrel with that approach since my third teacher, Samuel Margolis, also taught me to sing that way, to good effect. If you are able to produce beautiful, modified "ee" vowels in your upper range, well and good. Continue using them on the stage. But, as an exercise in the studio, you can strengthen your voice by mastering the unmodified "ee" throughout your entire range.

Remember, though, as you produce the unmodified "ee" in your upper range, a slight pinching sensation in the larynx is to be expected. This unmodified "ee" must be accompanied by a strong Support/Appoggio—in other words, a strong compression between the diaphragm and the support muscles, in lieu of a compression under the vocal folds. If the sound breaks or gets scratchy as you ascend in pitch, it is probably because you have not kept the breath pressure sufficiently away from the vocal folds.

It might also be that you are trying to *pull* the high notes up into the mask, as though "high" had something to do with the direction of "up." That, of course, is false! "High" refers to the high frequency of sound waves, not to the direction of "up." Are high notes on the piano up above the keyboard? Of course not! They are off to the right—not up. Forget the word "high" when speaking of the voice. Get smart like the Italians and think "acute notes" (note acute) instead of "high notes."

When you employ this "unmodified ee-track" correctly there is absolutely no sensation of placement above the vocal folds throughout your entire range. As you ascend in pitch the vocal folds will draw a little more tightly together, tending to elevate the breath pressure from below and tempting one to push the sound "higher" with the breath. On the contrary, the feeling should be that of a sharp razor slicing downward between the vocal folds. Higher, in this case, actually means a deeper, narrower sound accompanied by a stronger feeling of compression between the support muscles and the diaphragm. This compression should be felt in the region of the solar plexus. And never forget there must be *absolutely no sensation of placement of the tone above the vocal folds.*

As you ascend in pitch, there must be no widening of the lips, no spreading of the naso-pharynx, no extra opening of the jaw, and absolutely no facial contortions (including wrinkling the forehead and raising the eyebrows). The sound must be produced entirely in and by the larynx, accompanied by the slight pinching sensation mentioned before. This exercise, when properly employed throughout one's entire vocal range, strengthens the laryngeal muscles and serves to detach and loosen the jaw.

The Unmodified "Oo" in the Third-Voice

The same strengthening effect of the unmodified "ee" vowel can also be found using its parallel, the unmodified "oo" vowel, which is a form of the first-voice.

Proper production of the unmodified "oo" in the male's upper voice is best found by attacking a high note with the syllable, "noo". But the "oo" must be spaced very small and felt just beneath the front of the tongue. The "unmodified oo-track" is distinctly different from that of the fundamental-third-voice, which provides a roomy sensation of spacing deep in the throat.

As this exercise is mastered all the way up to the highest notes in the male singer's voice, the low and middle voice will become richer and easier.

Conclusion

Women often encounter some weakness in the third-voice when coming up out of the second-voice, which they call chest. This weakness comes from not shifting the resonance from the dome of the hard palate to the region behind and under the back of the tongue, when using the fundamental-third-voice with its shoehorn effect. It is a mistake to prematurely attempt to place the notes in this range "up and over," or "behind the eyeballs," which is only proper for the still higher range of the fourth-voice.

What strengthens the female's voice in the beginning of this range is making a slightly nasalized sound that is firmly kept down in the larynx through the gagging position, or shoehorn effect. Think of making the sound of an old-fashioned police siren, which is a deep, brilliant nasal sound. This is an approach that wipes out obvious register changes for both men and women in the range immediately above middle C.

Now a valid question can be asked, "Should one expect the female voice to operate on exactly the same principles as the male voice?" I fully believe the answer to be "Yes!"

A confusion often arises when a woman is instructing a male singer in the placement of his high voice. There is a tendency to mistakenly think that placement of the high voice should be treated exactly the same for both men and women. The error creeps in from assuming that the male high voice is the same thing as the female high voice. Actually, the male high voice (the third-voice) is the female's middle voice and has a deep production associated with the shoehorn effect, whereas the female's high voice has a production associated with a high placement behind the eyeballs.

Yes, men's and women's voices are basically the same, but we have confused the terminology when discussing their registers. When the woman says "chest" the male is saying "middle." When the woman says "high," the male says "falsetto." When the male says "high" the woman says "middle." If that is not enough to drive one up the wall, what is?

Now, back to similarities. Consider the difficulty that plagues most male singers when they approach the high, or third-voice. For basses the problem begins on the D-natural just above middle C; for baritones on the E-natural above that; for the tenor it usually begins around the F-sharp. Now, consider what happens with women's voices in that same range just above middle C. It is usually their most problematic range. This is not just a coincidence, it is the result of men and women both having the same four voices with which to deal.

If a man develops his fourth-voice, he will find that the placement up behind the eyeballs, which is natural to the woman when she isolates her fourth-voice, is also natural to him in that upper range (a range that he does not employ in his ordinary course of singing).

When he goes to the upper limit of his fourth-voice he finds that, in a manner similar to the coloratura soprano, he can add several notes to his high range by shifting to the falsettone or first-voice.

A young dramatic soprano, who was enrolled as a Fellow in Opera Music Theatre International, was gifted with extraordinary range, agility and divine pianissimos. In one of our concerts she experienced some problems in singing a difficult aria. Her low voice was unpleasantly muddy, which distinctly detracted from an otherwise beautiful performance.

The following week, I sat with her and discussed the problem. When she descended from her middle, or third-voice, into what she, like all women, calls her chest voice, she tried to maintain the deep placement of her third-voice and the result was a muddy

86

sound. Now, the third-voice placement for both male and female singers is deep down under the back of the tongue. But for male and female singers, the second-voice has to be shifted back up into the dome of the hard palate.

This soprano was trying to stay in "one gear" during this transition. The thought that she was going into what women call "chest" falsely lead her to think even deeper in the throat, when she should have "shifted gears" and placed the sound "up" in the dome of her hard palate.

Now, she is a very bright young lady and it did not take more than a few minutes for the truth to set in. During the following week, we put her on the stage in a 2,900 seat hall and had her do the aria again. This time, the result was beautiful singing throughout her entire range.

Some people object to the idea that there are distinctly different registers in the human voice. Object they may, but the registers are there and the transitions between them can sometimes be quite problematic. The challenge is to make the transitions so smooth that one is not aware of them.

The most difficult transition for most singers, both male and female, is the one which lies between the second- and third-voices, all within the first half of an octave above middle C. It is easily smoothed out by using a slightly nasal placement in the transition itself. The pivot note that lies exactly between the second and third registers, when produced with this tinge of nasality, is called a "mixed tone" or "misto."

A very simple trick to help iron out overt transitions is to make like an old fashioned police siren throughout the first three voices. Of course, that is a bright, but deep, nasal sound produced without lingering on any individual pitch: the sound must slur throughout. When properly done, you can go through your entire range without the slightest sign of a transition.

Even though registers are for real, one must employ the voice in such a manner that the transitions between them virtually are imperceptible. Keep this prominently in mind as you go through this analysis of the four voices.

CHAPTER X

THE FOURTH-VOICE

The female's high range is what we will call the "fourth-voice," and is best described as a "supported falsetto." Placement associated with the fourth-voice is up high in back of the nasal cavities, resonating behind the eyeballs. The optimum placement of the fourth-voice is commonly described as "up and over," and the external sign of its employment is commonly seen in a raising of the singer's eyebrows.

Although the fourth-voice is only occasionally employed by male singers for comic effect, I strongly recommend that all of them pay serious attention to what follows in this chapter.

When a man vocalizes in the fourth-voice he should imitate the full and brilliant sound of the female opera singer's higher range, a bright and crystalline sound, ample in volume. As the sound originates over and behind the eyeballs, it should feel as though it were being drawn out of the throat from above, completely abandoning the shoehorn effect of the third-voice.

When the male singer regularly exercises his fourth-voice, his normal singing range soon becomes clearer and more brilliant in color, and he spontaneously feels more like singing. This is a very positive effect; so much so, that many singers, both male and female, advocate using this placement exclusively throughout their entire vocal range. But such an approach ultimately proves to be much too restrictive.

Although singing in such a manner in the lower range produces a clear sound, it is a sound robbed of its full potential richness. So, when singing in any range below that of the fourth-voice, placement should not be exclusively held "up and over" behind the eyeballs, but should be varied according to the range involved. This is true for men and women alike.

Speaking from personal experience, during occasional performances in which I tried to place my voice exclusively "up and over," my wife, Lucia would come running backstage complaining with, "Darleeng, what you are doing? That ees only half your voice."

I have known quite a few male soloists who relied very heavily on the high resonance just described and every one of them was an excellent singer whose voice was superb on recordings. But their voices were too light for the big houses and they could not compete with the real heavyweights on the opera stage.

Any female singer that tries to keep her voice placed exclusively up behind her eyeballs throughout her entire range is going to possibly end up with a heroic high voice that is weak in the middle and low. Instead, she must shift to a deeper placement with a strong emphasis on the shoehorn effect for the middle voice, and again shift to the front of the mouth for her so-called chest voice.

As I already said, the trouble with isolating and using just the fourth-voice is that it does not add "brilliance" to the voice, but robs it of the lower resonances when singing in the ranges best served by the first-, second- or third-voices. A complete voice is one that has both the depth *and* brightness that is found by judiciously exercising all of the voices, including the fourth.

Next let us turn our attention to welding all four voices into one.

CHAPTER XI

THE FOUR VOICES AS ONE

We will begin this chapter from the viewpoint of the male singer and then continue it from the female singer's perspective. Whereas we have dedicated ourselves to isolating the four voices in the previous four chapters, we now seek to weld them back together again into what sounds like one voice.

First-Voice To Second

As we have already indicated, if the male singer basically employs a laryngeal style of singing, using unmodified vowels throughout his entire range, there will be no basic challenge of consolidating different "voices" into one, since there will be no change of registers to deal with. (I previously went on record as saying that this is a riskier way of singing and must be approached cautiously, requiring real intelligence on the singer's part as well as skillful teaching. But bear in mind that many great singers have come from this school of singing, so it is well worth our consideration.)

I, instead, recommend an approach based upon the three fundamental-voices, which are richer and warmer in sound than that produced by the laryngeal school. The opposite extreme of the narrow vowels of the laryngeal school is achieved by using the shoehorn effect, or gagging position, throughout one's entire range. When the "oo" vowel, for example, is produced in such a manner, it is based deep in the throat, resulting in a lowered larynx with a feeling of a round spacing under the tongue. This is the opposite sensation from that of the unmodified "ee" and "oo" vowels, which are placed well forward under the front of the jaw.

In contrast, when employing the fundamental-first-voice, the "oo" should be perceived as a floating ball of sound under the vocal folds. When employing the fundamental-second-voice, the "oo" should be perceived as a ball of sound being drawn from above and filling the dome of the hard palate—still maintaining the deep rooting of the shoehorn effect in the larynx. When shifting to the fundamental-third-voice, the "oo" vowel's floating ball of sound correspondingly shifts back into the rear of the naso-pharynx without abandoning the shoehorn effect deep in the larynx. And one must still maintain the sensation of drawing the sound out of the throat from above.

All vowels should be treated exactly in this manner, while continually maintaining the shoehorn effect. There is also a change in the use of the breath when going from the first-voice to the second-voice. When using the first-voice, with its rumbling feeling in the chest, the breath must literally be blown out through the vocal folds.

After ascending about halfway through the first-voice, the singer can begin to shift to a sensation of drawing the sound up out of the throat into the dome of the hard palate. When he reaches the transition to the second-voice, the singer should feel as though his vocal folds were now located in the dome of the hard palate, with the sound originating there, instead of under the sternum. Here one encounters a sensation often likened to a "soap bubble in the mouth," or simply a "mouthful of sound."

Let us once again resort to the imagery of a ball bouncing on top of a fountain of water. When employing the fundamental-first-voice, the ball can be imagined to be floating just under the sternum and, when shifting to the fundamental-second-voice, the ball can be imagined to be floating in the dome of the hard palate.

Second-Voice To Third

When dealing with the third-voice in Chapter IX, we discussed the imageries of the shoehorn, the fat end of the pear and also the long balloon, all of which lead to a sensation of placement deep in the back of the throat. In this major transition from the second to the third-voice, all the vowels are somewhat modified, with the change in the "ah" vowel being the most drastic, going to "uh" (as in "up").

However drastic this transition, it can be considerably eased by employing, in addition to the shoehorn effect, a bit of nasality as one approaches and enters the range of the third-voice.

When completely in the third-voice, *all* sensation of a forward placement in the mouth shifts back until it feels as though the sound were going straight out the top of one's head. But remember that in the third-voice, one must continue to employ the shoehorn effect.

Third-Voice To Fourth

We must now revert to discussing the female voice. Keep in mind that what the woman calls chest voice is the male's middle voice, or the second-voice, and what the woman calls her middle voice is the male's high voice, or the third-voice. Everything said about the male's placement for the first-, second- and third-voices will apply equally well to the woman's voice. The same is true for the transition between the woman's first three voices.

As the female ascends from the third-voice to the fourth-voice, the ball of sound should slowly ascend up the back of the throat until it feels exclusively lodged up behind the eyeballs. However, this involves a register change in the neighborhood of the second D to F above the middle C, which can be really problematic for some singers. It is especially challenging for those with heavier voices such as dramatic sopranos and mezzos, who often tend to have pitch problems there.

Marilyn Horne likens this passage between the third and fourth-voices to an "hourglass" or "two pyramids" placed tip to tip, one above the other. In other words there should be a narrowing sensation when going from the third to the fourth-voices or vice versa.

As we said in the previous chapter, the placement of the fourth-voice is frequently described as "singing back, up and over." There should be no sensation of singing in the throat as is the case with the third-voice. The "ball floating on the fountain" should now be imagined as located just above and behind the eyes, in what women describe as the "mask."

When descending from the fourth-voice to the third-voice, we can use the imagery of an ostrich swallowing an apple, which would parallel the sensation of the "ball of sound" descending from behind the eyeballs down into the throat. But it must include the sensation of narrowing between the two registers.

As we have previously noted, it is not uncommon for female singers, when going up in pitch from their so-called chest voice (second-voice) to develop a weakness before getting fully into their head voice (fourth-voice). This is probably the result of going from the placement belonging to her so-called chest voice (third-voice) directly to the placement belonging to her head voice (fourth-voice), which means she is skipping the approach that works naturally for her middle voice, based upon the shoehorn effect. Putting the sound up behind the eyeballs in the third-voice does not work well.

Focus
Although I have employed what is called "focus" on various occasions, I do not generally use it.

Some singers employ focus, or "tubing it," to smooth out the transition between the first-, second- and third-voices. The sensation of focus begins in the front of the mouth and can be described as follows:

Touch the ends of all your fingers and thumb of one hand like a closed tulip bulb and then imagine your entire hand being enclosed in a rubber sleeve. With the thumb underneath and the fingertips above, slowly expand your fingers and thumb like a blossoming flower. Then imagine the resultant combination of "gentle force and resistance" that would ensue. This "blossom of sound" describes the sensation of "focus" and should feel like a "ball of sound" in the front of the mouth.

When going from the upper half of the first-voice to the lower half of the second-voice, focus can help to knit the two voices together. When doing this, the blossom, or ball of sound should be felt exclusively in the front of the mouth, just behind the upper and lower teeth. The result should be a sensation of having lifted the voice entirely out of the throat, placing it in the front of the mouth.

When employing focus there is often a tendency to protrude the lips to enhance the sensation. Now, there is no great harm in doing this, but it is unnecessary and should be avoided if possible.

It is not necessary to employ focus in the lower half of the first-voice, although it can be used. Actually, the best results are achieved in the very low voice with complete relaxation and no sensation of focus or placement in the mouth or the mask.

Let us now discuss how focus can be used in the transition from the second-voice to the third-voice: Continuing with the imagery of the "rubber sleeve," when one enters the upper half of the second-voice and begins to shift into the third-voice, the sensation of focus will shift back from the front of the mouth and move down deep into the throat, until it is felt that the expanding fingers and thumb are now in the region of the vocal folds.

Now one should feel the "blossom," or "ball of sound" in the region where the vocal folds are located. In other words, the "ball of sound" has now shifted back down from the front of the mouth where it was originally felt. One should feel a sensation of spacing under the tongue where the floating ball should now be located.

Falsettone and Whistle Tones

As was previously noted in Chapter VI, when both men and women take the fourth-voice to its highest extremes, resorting to the pinch effect, the falsettone, or the whistle tone enables the singer to add a few more notes to the high range. The rather astonishing conclusion that we reached was that the stratospheric high notes of the coloratura soprano are fundamentally first-voice which is true chest-voice.

Now, this phenomenon is not exclusively reserved for the coloratura soprano, but is a property common to all male and female voices. Any man, properly producing the highest notes in his fourth-voice, will find he can go a little higher by switching to the narrow, deep and pinched production of the falsettone.

When some women sing in the upper extremes of their high voices they have a tendency to spread the sound with a widening of the mouth and the naso-pharynx. This can be corrected by leaning in the direction of the deeper placed whistle tones. But this must be accompanied by a strong feeling of smiling under the sternum.

Conclusion

As an exercise, I recommend that all male singers strive to make a full sound in the fourth-voice, imitating the female opera singer in that range, and then try to descend smoothly down through the third-, second- and first-voices, using the shoehorn effect continuously after leaving the fourth-voice. But bear in mind that there should be a smooth transition between the four voices, and that certain throat settings are essential to accomplishing this.

When coming down from the "high female" or fourth-voice, a male singer will commonly find a break between his fourth-voice and his own natural high or third-voice. This is the same problematic register change that can plague women with heavier voices. Such a problem can be overcome by exaggerating the feeling of the shoe-horn effect during the transition into the third-voice and relying on the "hourglass" effect described earlier. The placement should settle down into the back of the throat and the "ah" vowel should tend toward "uh". This will facilitate a smooth transition between the fourth and third-voices.

When shifting from the third-voice to the second-voice, men and women alike will profit by switching from the spacing in the back of the throat to the spacing in the dome of the hard palate. As we noted before, this can be accomplished without a trace of register change by producing the critical passaggio notes slightly nasally.

Then, when descending into the first-voice, all sensation of placement above the vocal folds should be abandoned and more breath should be fed through them. At this point, it helps to imagine a sensation of a spacing that descends down behind the tongue and curls up in front under it. This procedure should enable any singer to go through a total range of at least three and a half octaves.

For the male singer, I recommend that all vowel sounds through-out the entire range should feel as though they were fastened down deep and back through the shoehorn effect, together with the sensations of placement and breath discussed above.

As I stated previously, an even greater range can be achieved by starting on top with the falsettone or first-voice, better achieved with an unmodified "ee" vowel, which enables one to begin almost a half an octave higher than is possible with the fourth-voice. But to preserve a smooth continuity when descending in pitch, one should remain in the first-voice, using the pinch effect all the way down to the lowest notes in one's range.

This sort of challenge for all voices will enable a singer to find his/her complete voice, and will tend to wipe out any obvious switching of gears when going from one register to another.

I know this will sound controversial to many, but it is not theory, it may be demonstrated practically. However, in my own case, it took me almost fifty years to accomplish what we have just discussed, because it was "What My Teachers Never Taught Me."

P.S. There is a chart in Appendix II which clearly delineates the differences in terminology used by male and female singers.

CHAPTER XII

THE LESSON

I have always been too busy performing to be tied down as a voice instructor. Teaching a beginning student requires three voice lessons a week during the first few years of training and I have not been in a position to provide any such continuity.

Instead of calling myself a teacher, I consider myself to be a trouble-shooter for the professional level singer. In this chapter, I will describe the type of lesson that I give to those who are capable of profiting from a limited number of sessions, focusing on the problems and flaws that I commonly encounter, together with the solutions I have found to be effective. I also hope that this chapter will be as valuable to the teacher as it will be to the student.

Determining Voice Categories
Through the Opera Music Theatre International (OMTI)

program in Newark, New Jersey, I have had occasion to hear over 2,000 auditions, mostly in a 2,900 seat auditorium. One interesting fact has emerged: approximately one singer in four is singing in the wrong vocal category. The problem is that singing in a category one level too low can produce really virtuoso results, but only in the "little-league."

But when that singer tries to compete in the "big-league," where international careers are being made, he/she simply cannot stand up against the vocal heavyweights that grand opera requires.

Now, if you are teaching a basso cantante, make sure he is just that. Unfortunately, nine out of ten basso cantantes that I hear turn out to be baritones who have never learned to sing their high notes properly. So, how does one discern the difference?

A true basso cantante can usually sustain a good open "ah" vowel on the D-natural above middle C (some basses can do a decent open "ah" on E-flat). But, if the singer can produce a good sounding open "ah" vowel on the E-natural, then without question, he is a baritone.

The basso cantante should also be able to effectively cover the "ah" vowel on the D-natural without sounding crimped. Whether the D-natural should be open or covered should depend entirely on the phrase and its mood. But the ability to do it either way is essential. In addition, a good technician should also be able to sing a D-natural with the "misto," or "mixed tone" that we have adequately defined in Chapter IX.

The first D-natural above middle C is the pivotal note for the true basso cantante, and can be problematic until its production is thoroughly mastered.

The first E-natural above middle C is the pivotal note for the true baritone. Should the singer be able to produce a good sounding open "ah" vowel on the F-natural above middle C, you probably have a tenor on your hands.

The first F-sharp above middle C is the common pivotal note for the tenor, although the pivotal note for the dramatic tenor can be as low as F-natural. The corresponding pivotal note for most higher and lighter tenor voices is G-natural. To allow tenors to open the "ah" vowel above G-natural is tempting fate.

The means of determining a viable classification for women's voices is similar to this, but I will leave the details to the women who have more in-depth experience with training the female voice than I do.

The Singing Lesson for the Male

In the early seventies, the *New York Times* interviewed Dorothy Kirsten, Robert Merrill and me on the subject of our longevity at the Met. Each of us had sung there for thirty years. I felt it was not a coincidence that two of us, Bob and I, had studied for years with the same teacher, Samuel Margolis. He had trained us on fast moving scales, designed to produce the big sound with maximum flexibility, which probably accounted for the fact that both of us endured on the stage with fresh sounding voices for such a long time.

Therefore, I usually begin my first session with a singer by explaining that most of what we are about to do will be based upon fast moving scales in which the individual notes will be divided by a slight impulse, almost like a "half-h". I aim for maximum speed as well as maximum volume. The purpose of this is to prepare a voice that will be rich in sound, yet extremely flexible. Such an approach will hopefully guarantee a fresh and youthful voice for many, many years.

I usually begin a basso's lesson with the following warm up exercise:

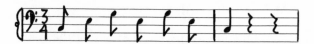

Bee, bee, bee, bee, bee, bee, bee___

For the basso, I begin on the second A-flat below middle C and work up by half steps until the high note is the first E-/F-natural above middle C. I then return down by half steps until the low note is the second E-natural below middle C.

103

For the baritone, I duplicate the above a whole tone higher, with the highest note ending on the first G-natural above middle C.

For the tenor, I start a whole tone higher and continue on up to at least the high B-flat.

In doing this arpeggio, I do not allow the student to indulge in any facial contortions while singing in the high range. Raising the eyebrows, or wrinkling the forehead indicates that the singer is incorrectly associating high notes with an increasingly higher feeling of placement in the mask. And spreading the mouth laterally generally indicates a lateral spreading of the naso-pharynx, which is anathema.

I have nothing against modifying the "ee" vowel to "ih" when performing on the stage. But, for this warm-up, I require the student to employ the unmodified "ee" throughout the entire range, which means that there should be absolutely no increased opening of the jaw with higher pitch.

In the next exercise, I use the following scale:

Mee--------------------Ah----------------------

Meh--------------Ah----------------------

This exercise is to be employed throughout the entire range at maximum speed, making sure that all notes are cleanly separated with gentle impulses from the diaphragm, but not sung staccato. Be sure all notes are given equal duration and stress. The notes are to resemble the proverbial string of *matching* pearls. No one note is to be given a greater emphasis or importance than another.

It is particularly important to carefully monitor the "ah" vowel on the descending scales to make sure that the first and fifth notes are not stressed when coming down, carefully avoiding any distortion of the vowel. This will help guarantee an even column of sound throughout the entire vocal range, eliminating the impression that one is passing from one register to another.

A common flaw is the tendency to go from the "ee" vowel to the "ah" vowel by punching the attack on the "ah". This occurs because the "ee" is produced with a relatively closed position of the jaw (if produced correctly), whereas the "ah" vowel is sung with an open position of the jaw. Making a precipitous change in the jaw position is the cause of this problem and should be avoided. With a proper impulse between these notes this problem will not occur.

The male singers should start out on the above scale, beginning on the lowest comfortable note, and continuing to raise the scale a half note at a time until the highest note in the scale is a half tone above the pivotal note. Keep the "ah" vowel on the passing note open. I then begin moving the scale one half tone lower each time until we reach the lowest comfortable note in the singer's range.

On occasion, you can venture all the way up to the highest part of the singer's range. But, all "ah" vowels sung a whole tone above the pivotal note are to be covered.

Please carefully note that I advocate singing the "ah" vowels completely open on passing notes up to and including a half tone above the pivotal tone, but not—I repeat—not on sustained notes.

The next scale I employ is a bit more difficult:

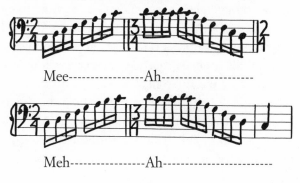

Mee----------------Ah--------------------

Meh----------------Ah------------------------

The three turns on the high note often tend to become clumsy. The singer will either slow up on the turn, or will lose the impulse and make a somewhat drunken slur. The problem usually becomes acute when the turn is in the neighborhood of the pivotal note. Singers can seek the solution to this clumsiness even when working without the teacher, since it does not require a second ear to tell them when they are not doing it well.

The range employed in this scale is exactly the same as that of the previous one.

The next scale is yet more difficult:

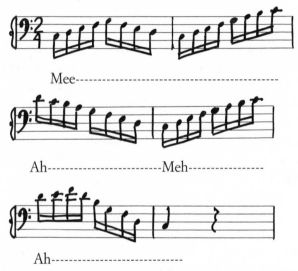

This scale should always encompass the entire range of the voice, even going as far up as a whole tone above the highest note the singer commonly employs on the stage. When negotiating the highest parts of this scale, be careful to keep clear impulses between the notes, especially the three highest ones. And do not allow the highest note to be punched or held longer than the others: it must just be another note and not be given any special distinction.

A good variation of this scale is to repeat the fourth and fifth bars as many times as one can. On a good day, I have managed to do it seven times. The more agile voices can do an even greater number of repetitions. One of my OMTI tenors from Beijing, China, Jing-Ma Fan, managed to do it twelve times! Now, that is a feat! I then take the singer into the high range, using:

Mah------------------------

I then vary this with:

Mee------------------------

In the following arpeggio, I insist on the student using the unmodified "ee" vowel. If you wish to hear a somewhat more beautiful sound, the "ee" can be somewhat modified by thinking of "smiling under the sternum." In performance, one can modify the "ee" vowel according to one's taste. But using the unmodified "ee" in this arpeggio builds a much stronger first-voice, which is one's vocal foundation. *This is for a muscle builder, not a beauty contest.*

Again, do not allow any facial contortions when employing this arpeggio. Make the singer look in a mirror in stubborn cases.

This exercise is of special importance since it requires the student to do equally well in singing both the "ee" and "ah" vowels in the high voice. This leads to the singer being comfortable on all vowels in the upper range, which is usually a real challenge. Through variations of the following arpeggio on different vowels, the student can become comfortable in employing all the vowels, "ee", "ey", "eh", "oo", "oh" and "ah" in the high voice:

107

Mee-----------------------Mah--------------------

This scale is to be sung as quickly as possible, and again with no facial contortions. The configurations of the jaw, tongue and naso-pharynx to form the "ee" and "ah" vowels are each set on the lowest note and should not change in anyway throughout the entire range.

The following scale is quite useful in developing the mezza voce:

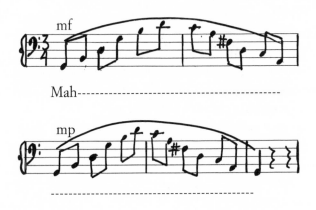

Mah---

The first two bars are sung forte and the rest piano.

Most male singers find that singing high notes usually requires more effort than singing in the middle voice. This is not necessary. The following scale is excellent for training the singer to find a high voice that feels as easy as middle voice:

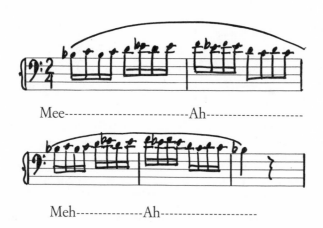

Mee------------------------Ah---------------------

Meh--------------Ah---------------------

When this scale is used in the high range, the male singer must completely abandon any sensation of placement in the mask and resort to the third-voice, which feels as though the sound were being produced deep in the throat, with a spacing below the back of the tongue in the region of the vocal folds. This is not to be confused with the first-voice, which in one modification bears a distinct pinch-feeling in the larynx. This third-voice approach must leave the throat feeling like an empty pipe. And the sound must feel as though it were being drawn up out of the throat, not driven from below.

When properly employed, the highest part of this exercise will become very easy and you will feel as though you were singing with the middle-voice. If, however, you were to try to use this approach in your middle range, it would give you a muddy sound.

I usually return to the second exercise given in this lesson, just to cool the voice off.

Testing and Conditioning the Voice

Most singers resort to "tricks of the voice" when testing the voice's condition or when the voice is not in good shape. This can be of particular importance if you are in a location where there is not a laryngologist who is experienced in dealing with opera singers.

These "tricks" are a departure from strict vocal exercises and are usually individual tricks that various singers have found effective.

One of the most common tricks used to test the condition of the male voice is to sing a high, light, unsupported falsetto. If an easy falsetto is not there, you are not in good voice and probably should have a bit of vocal rest.

If, in bringing that unsupported falsetto down to the middle singing range, there is not a smooth, unbroken sound, there is probably some unevenness on the vocal folds. To be sure, take a look at them with your homemade laryngeal mirror, as will be suggested in Chapter XV.

I often test the condition of my voice by making sounds while inhaling. If the sound does not come easily, I am somewhat laryngitic.

A vocal trick used extensively by the Metropolitan Opera coloratura, Rita Shane, was to practice singing a high glissando, using the "falsettone" described in Chapter VII, which women commonly call a "whistle tone." This tests the clarity of the voice and also serves as a strengthener of the laryngeal muscles.

Richard Tucker was usually heard employing a vocal trick that goes with a Melocchi type of singing: a brilliant "zzee" in the high voice.

Regarding therapeutic tricks, one that was popular twenty years ago was the "chewing exercise." This is simply done by lightly singing:

Yum, yum, yum, yum, yum, yum,   yum.

It is purported to have therapeutic value for the voice.

If I am in rough voice, rolling the "r" is usually helpful in clearing the sound.

I also find it helpful to vocalize as follows:

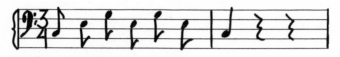

Lay, lay, lay, lay, lay, lay, lay.

making a simple baby type sound with no attempt to color or place the sound. When in good voice, you should be able to do this arpeggio throughout your entire range.

If I have a scratch on a particular note in some part of my voice, I take the falsetto sound two octaves above, which usually seems to have the same sort of scratch, and play around with that note, gently increasing its intensity and volume, until the scratch disappears.

Of course, these are tricks and have little to do with vocal techniques to be used in singing. You probably have some personal tricks of your own. If not, play around and find some.

CHAPTER XIII

CHOOSING A TEACHER

I shall open this discussion by doing something very unpopular: I am going to defend the teacher! In spite of the fact that any dilettante or charlatan can pose as a teacher—and I have known many such—there are also many pedagogues who deserve to be defended. Almost every time a student fails the blame is laid on the teacher. And, when a student succeeds, it is said to be "in spite of the teacher." This mindset is very real—and very unfair. There are many aspiring singers out there who will be *destroyed* by any hapless teacher who has the misfortune to let them in the door. The sad part is that the teacher will get all of the blame for this self-destructive songbird.

Let me recount an incident that occurred early in 1949, across the street from Carnegie Hall. I had just switched voice teachers, leaving Rocco Pandiscio after two years of study, and had begun working with Robert Merrill's teacher, Samuel Margolis. That particular spring day, as I left my new Maestro's studio, I was confronted by a young bass, one of the few in New York tall enough to eyeball it with me.

"I hear you are studying with Margolis," he stated accusingly.

"Yep," I responded, as coolly as a professional gunslinger in a Grade-B-Western.

"You know he was ruining my voice...!"

"Yep!"

Two months before my defection to Margolis, I sat in · Pandiscio's studio as this young man auditioned. He sang quite poorly and under questioning by the Maestro disclosed that he was a pupil of Margolis. At the mention of that name, Pandiscio rolled his eyes in abject disapproval, declaring that Margolis was ruining his voice. Now, it had been my experience that everyone who auditioned for Pandiscio was being ruined by his/her teacher. One came away from the Pandiscio studio with the distinct impression that this was the last bastion of truth in the opera world, and that wisdom would die with him.

"You still intend to study with Margolis, knowing that he was ruining my voice?" my accuser demanded aggressively.

"Yep!"

"I guess I'd better start learning your repertoire," he said and his meaning was clear enough.

"Well," I said, "I hope, for your sake, that he will promptly ruin my voice and open the door for your career."

Thus ended our acidulous encounter. As time passed, I so profited by working with Margolis that I continued working with him for more than twenty-five years. In retrospect, the young bass who had confronted me was certainly on the wrong vocal track and Margolis was taking the blame. In contrast, his pupil, Robert Merrill, sang beautifully and everyone said it was "in spite of Margolis."

Most people cannot learn to sing well without formal training. There are rare exceptions to this rule, but I surely was not one of them, and I don't advocate going it alone. I feel that even the few successful singers who claim to be self-taught could have profited by having a good teacher. Ah, but what constitutes a good teacher?

Bear in mind that a so-called good teacher might not be good for some pupils. The ultimate question is "What constitutes a good student-teacher relationship?" Some people work well together and some do not. If you are looking for a good teacher, first make sure that you are a good pupil. With that in mind, let us discuss what one should look for in a good teacher, and what pitfalls one should avoid.

First, let us consider how one becomes a teacher of voice. There are several routes by which one may achieve this:

1) *The teacher is an academic.*
2) *The teacher studied to be an opera singer, but never reached the professional stage.*
3) *The teacher sang professionally for a few years, possibly as a leading soloist in major houses.*
4) *The teacher had a long, successful singing career.*
5) *The teacher never formally studied voice, but has been an accompanist or a singing coach.*

Good teachers can come from any one of these five categories, but each category will have its own built-in problems. Let us analyze these categories in depth:

1) The teacher is an academic.
A teacher who is an academic will be better versed than most on textbooks concerning vocal technique, from Lamperti to Vennard, and will be well schooled, musically, possibly with a major in voice and a minor in piano. There will probably be a Master's degree in teaching hanging on the wall. Your teacher will be well informed on the history of music and be a good sightreader. All of these are accomplishments to be admired and valued, but the big question is:

115

What does your teacher really know about training an operatic voice for the great stages of the world?

Undoubtedly, this teacher will have heard most of the world's greatest vocalists on records, on television and live in major theaters. But, there is one problem: has that teacher ever spent an extensive amount of time in a small room, or studio, working up close with world-class voices? Probably not. Does that teacher, as the personal friend of successful opera singers, have the opportunity to discuss, on a one-on-one basis, the problems a performer faces in the real world, and how they are resolved? Probably not. Do the teacher and pupil have access to a large auditorium for advanced training? Probably not.

The first major problem that can arise from having such a teacher is that he/she has no way of knowing what a really world-class voice sounds like in the studio. Disastrous judgment calls are often made. How often have I been invited to someone's studio to hear the world's next great Otello, only I hear, instead, some kid that should be singing Count Almaviva. In the studio he sounds impressive. In a big hall he would disappear.

Half of the students I hear today are singing the wrong repertoire, and many are actually in the wrong voice category. They get away with singing the wrong things for a long time since they only sing in the studio or smaller theaters. With my Opera Music Theatre International in New Jersey, we have auditioned 2,000 professional-level singers in a hall which seats almost 3,000. Impressive voices, that I had personally heard in a studio, often crashed in the big hall. The problem was usually caused by singing the wrong repertoire, and it would not become evident until the singer set foot on a large stage.

My first teacher, Gennaro Curci, used to hire a major theater in Los Angeles to present his students in "The Curci Opera Workshop." At the age of eighteen, I sang Mephistopheles in the second act of *Faust* at the Ebell Theatre in Los Angeles. Curci rightly maintained that the theater was the greatest teacher of all, and through him I had the golden opportunity to discover how different it was to sing in a large hall.

Another serious problem stems from academia. Ruth Dobson, head of the opera department of Portland State University, summed it up when she said to me:

"I have a confession to make. I'm afraid that we academics may be destroying a whole generation of young singers. We are afraid to make them sound like opera singers because we fear that if they hurt their little voices we will lose our jobs."

I am happy to report that Ruth has built a highly professional voice department which turns out first class singers. But on a national scale the basic problem still remains, some of it caused by the absurd increase in frivolous lawsuits.

A phrase we used to hear forty years ago, "If, by an act of God..." is no longer acceptable because today's "legal eagles" can't sue God and collect. So America's flawed court system encourages legal extortion through quick settlements of trivial suits, a game which has become as popular as playing the lottery. It puts the poor teacher in a serious bind, but it is the pupil who suffers in the end.

Consider a twenty-year-old soprano who shows up in class with a big, gutsy voice. She wants to sing Verdi or Wagner, and she is probably right in wanting to do so. The teacher's guarded reaction is usually:

"Oh, my dear, you are much too young to even consider that sort of repertoire. You must gradually mature into it. Wait until you are thirty or thirty-five before you even think of it. You must grow like a flower, starting from a tiny bud. Begin by working on art songs and Mozart arias."

This is the worst thing one could do to that precocious prodigy. You don't become a dramatic soprano. Either you are born one or you aren't. To force a naturally dramatic voice to draw back into lighter repertoire is much like driving a high-powered racing car with both the accelerator and the brake pushed to the floor. You will burn out the motor.

117

Richard Tucker had a gutsy, dramatic voice. The heavy roles were easy for him. Dramatic roles came much more naturally to him from his earliest years. It was only in his more mature years that he ventured into the lighter repertoire. One of his great challenges was to sing delicately and softly in the lyric roles. As America's greatest tenor, he was determined to master all phases of his craft. I did Sarastro to his first Tamino in *The Magic Flute*, and he was justifiably proud when he mastered it.

You can ruin a heroic voice by prematurely whittling it down in size. Let the student do what comes naturally. What, then, should a twenty-year-old dramatic soprano be studying—art songs? What is she preparing to be, a lieder singer or an opera singer? Surely an opera singer should eventually become a good recitalist: I have personally sung 1,500 concerts in addition to my operatic career. But I learned my first art songs after I had already begun singing at the Metropolitan Opera. Who is going to hire you to do recitals without the Met name, or that of New York City Opera? The simple fact of life is: one becomes an opera singer by singing opera, and I don't mean just singing arias, I mean singing operas in their entirety.

It is a disgrace to find twenty-five-year-old students with Master's degrees, who don't even have two complete operas in their repertoire. Gennaro Curci taught me the role of Don Basilio, in *The Barber of Seville*, as I was turning seventeen. By the time I was twenty, I knew twenty operas in the original languages. At that tender age, I had already debuted with the San Francisco Opera as Monterone in *Rigoletto* and Bitterolf in *Tannhauser*, singing on the same stage with Lawrence Tibbett, Lily Pons, Jan Peerce, Lauritz Melchior, Stella Roman and Alexander Kipnis. My conductors were Papi and Leinsdorf. Naturally, some people predicted that this prematurely exploited youngster wouldn't be singing in another five years. I don't know what I did wrong, but I'm still at it fifty-five years later.

My wife, known in the profession as Lucia Evangelista, had fifteen operas in her repertoire when she debuted as Mimi, in *La Boheme*, at the age of nineteen in Genoa's largest theater. Despite her early start, she continued with her inimitable vocal artistry for another thirty-four years. What shortened her career was not the teenage debut, but the care and nurture of our four sons.

I am well aware of the danger of exploiting young voices, but this is not what I am advocating. When I began singing the complete role of Mephistopheles in *Faust* at the age of twenty-two (bear in mind that I was involved in a full-time science curriculum at UCLA), I did not sing that role more than four or five times a year. Young singers must be handled with caution and wisdom, but they must get accustomed to singing in theaters as soon as possible, and in repertoire suited to their natural voices.

The first time I heard George London (then known as George Burnson), he was singing the Coronation scene from *Boris Godunov*, at the age of nineteen, in the Shrine Auditorium in Los Angeles, a theater with a seating capacity of 7,000. Four years later, he was the Valentine in my first *Faust* performances, again in major theaters. Singing on the big stages taught him he could not effectively sustain the tessitura of the pure baritone roles, and he soon began undertaking the in-between bass-baritone repertoire. He chose wisely and proved himself to be an extraordinary artist and vocal technician. It was tragic that health problems so abruptly terminated his illustrious career.

In conclusion, my advice to academics is: don't be afraid to allow a young singer to do and be what comes naturally. If, at an early age, there are the signs of a really dramatic voice, let it be what it was designed to be. Don't crimp it with an exclusive diet of Mozart and art songs. Leave that to the voices which are lighter by nature. Also, try to launch those careers a bit sooner. Today's students are entering the profession at least five years later than those of the past generation.

2) *The teacher studied to be an opera singer, but never reached the professional stage.*

My first two teachers had professional careers and I learned much from them. My third teacher, Samuel Margolis, had his vocal

119

folds accidentally scarred by a doctor's assistant in his student days and had to relinquish his ambition for an operatic career, yet he became one of the finest teachers of his day. His lack of professional experience was no handicap. He had been well trained and knew how to pass it on. I chose to study with him because of the singers he turned out, especially Robert Merrill, who never studied with another teacher. Bob's beautiful singing was the best recommendation of all.

3) The teacher sang professionally for a few years, possibly as a leading soloist in major houses.

There are several possible reasons why a teacher could have had a short career. The career might have been aborted by physical problems, or even emotional ones, which would have no bearing on an ability to teach. Often, however, a career is dramatically shortened by some basic vocal problem that was never successfully resolved during the performing years. Unfortunately, that unresolved vocal problem will most likely be passed on to the pupil. Even in such a case, the teacher-pupil relationship can still be fruitful if the pupil, by nature, does not have the same problem the teacher did.

My first two teachers, Curci and Pandiscio, both had limited careers, yet I learned a considerable amount from them. Curci, for example, sang several years with his famous sister-in-law, Amelita Galli-Curci. They both toured with Titta Ruffo's *Hamlet* company, and also sang in Caruso's debut season in Buenos Aires. When Galli-Curci had her phenomenal success with The Chicago Opera, she asked her brother-in-law to give up his limited singing career and become her full- time coach, so he made the crucial decision to give up performing and devote himself to Amelita's career. He later became the leading voice teacher and opera coach in Los Angeles.

Curci also had the advantage of knowing all of the important people in the opera business. During the eight years I studied with him prior to singing at the Met, he provided me with many invaluable contacts. I sang in his living room for such VIP's as Ezio Pinza, Salvatore Baccaloni, Tito Schipa and Gaetano Merola. These encounters proved most helpful to my career. It can be of inestimable value to you if your teacher has been active in the theater and can provide such contacts. But remember, good contacts are no substitute for good singing.

4) The teacher had a long and illustrious career.

The problem with these teachers is that it is possible they have never given serious thought to teaching during all of the years of performance, and have no idea how to verbalize their technique. Your "star" teacher may know what to do, but not how to explain it. Now, these successful singers are usually pretty smart, or they never would have made it in life as they did, and they are often capable of making the transition from performer to teacher, but it takes time and diligent study.

However, there are a few who do not successfully make this adjustment, and their voice lessons degenerate into "Let me show you how I did it." You then try to match your famous teacher's sounds and fail. A subtle atmosphere develops which degenerates into "Nobody can do it like I did." The lessons can lapse into a real competition between teacher and student, and the student usually loses.

5) The teacher may have never formally studied voice, but has been an accompanist or coach for singers.

This lack of formal voice training does not necessarily mean that this person cannot successfully teach you to sing. I know of many cases where this sort of pupil-teacher relationship has worked quite well. If such a person has, through personal contact with professional singers, developed an excellent ear for what is a good operatic sound, he/she will be well qualified to say, "That's better," or "That's worse." This person has become the singer's external, objective ear. One can learn in this manner, but it is almost like being self-taught. The only difference is that the singer, who is unable to accurately hear his or her own voice, is at least getting a second opinion, which can be quite helpful.

Bearing in mind that good teachers can come from all of these diverse backgrounds, how do you go about choosing one? First, inquire as to who their pupils are. If one or two really excellent singers have come out of that studio, the prognosis is good. Then ask those singers how much they feel they have acquired from that particular teacher.

Second, don't be impressed by a teacher who is just a good salesperson. Glibness is a poor substitute for the ability to teach. Let me describe a personal experience that is enlightening.

I visited a major university to give a master class. I arrived a half an hour early and had a chance to visit with the head of the voice department. He expounded profusely on the science of acoustics, the Venturi Effect, the anatomy of the larynx and the breathing apparatus. I was given the name of every muscle and cartilage that twitched when one sang. After thirty minutes of such profound vocal savvy, I felt about two inches tall. How pitifully little I knew about the functioning of my own voice.

Then, his pupils sang for me and, suddenly, I became ten feet tall. What I heard was a joke, a parody of good singing. The only thing that was twitching properly was my funny bone. I had to remind myself that it really wasn't funny at all: it was devastating for those young hopefuls who were being so hopelessly misled.

When I attended UCLA, I had the privilege of studying under Hans Reichenbach, who was considered the world's greatest authority on Probability Logic. He also happened to be devoted to ice skating. One day in class he said, "Scientifically speaking, you will skate perfectly if you make the vector sum of all the forces in your body pass directly through the point of contact between your skate and the ice." He then smiled at the class and wisely added, "But who can learn to skate like that?"

This simply tells us that a profound scientific analysis can be totally useless in the pragmatic learning experience. It sounds great, but so what?

Dear student, don't be suckered in by much erudite nonsense. Only the simple approach which helps you perform better is worth finding. Be pragmatic: theory has its place, but it is secondary to practical results. What, then, should one's approach be?

First, I advocate that men study with men and that women study with women. Now, this is not an ironclad rule, but it has some advantages. If I hear a man sing incorrectly, I not only know it is wrong, but I can empathize with him in my throat. I actually sense and feel what he is doing wrong and can imitate his defect. This is true whether he is a bass, baritone or tenor. I can empathize with each of these.

When a woman sings incorrectly, I know it is wrong, but I cannot easily imitate her defect. The best I can do with the female student is to say "yes" or "no." I can tell if what she is doing is better or worse, but I must basically leave it up to the pupil to come up with alternative ideas. I can be much more profoundly involved in exper-imental, creative teaching when working with a male student.

If a man studies with a woman teacher, the greatest problem can be in the handling of the high voice. Some women will confuse the concept of the female high voice with that of the male high voice, which is actually to be compared to her middle voice. But we have discussed this in depth in previous chapters.

The result is that some woman teachers have a poor under-standing of the critical vowel adjustment that must occur between the male's second- and third-voices. All male singers must make this vowel adjustment somewhere between D and G just above middle C. Without this transition, tenors will end up masquerading as lyric baritones, baritones will end up pretending to be bass-baritones, and basses, having nowhere else to go, will simply avoid their high notes or spend their whole life messing them up.

How many basses specialize in the Moussorgsky version of *Boris Godunov* because they cannot sing the high G-flats in the Monologue. But I have already discussed this adjustment in detail in Chapter IX. It is a great challenge for the woman teacher to get the male student past this hurdle, especially since she will find it difficult to demonstrate the proper way of doing it, even if she understands it.

There is a similar problem with a man teaching a woman to sing. The uncharted paths for most men lie in the region of the woman's high voice. The man is unaccustomed to facing the problems of the placement of the female's high voice and the sometimes difficult transition between the third and fourth-voices. When most men attempt to come down from a high supported falsetto, or fourth-voice, into the range of their lower voices, they have great difficulty in making a smooth transition. How, then, can they advise a woman struggling with that same upper register change?

Another important thing I would like to stress is that one's lessons should not be anarchic in character. By this, I mean that the teacher should have a basic routine of increasingly difficult scales and arpeggios which taper off at the end in a cooling down period. This set of exercises should be basically the same for each lesson. Yes, there can and should be occasional variations in the routine from day to day, but there must be a basic routine, a basic skeleton that is there at every lesson. This routine should run from twenty-five to thirty-five minutes.

When advanced students (which includes professionals) are away from their teachers, they should run through this set of exercises religiously at least every second day of their lives. Singers must not spend too much time in haphazard experimentation. You don't get up on the morning of a performance saying, "Let's see if my high C is there." No, you work up to it in your regular routine, and at some time of day that is proper for you. Allow your voice to wake up with increasingly difficult exercises in the order to which your voice is accustomed. Then, if your voice happens to be temporarily off track, it will automatically tend to return to the proper track to which it has become accustomed in working with your teacher. Like the horse that knows its way back to the stable, your voice zeros back into the right groove.

I consider having such a set of basic exercises a matter of prime importance. Certainly, if you are not doing any public performances for a while, you can afford to experiment with new ideas, but never on the day of a performance.

Also remember that, in actual performance, your emotions, necessary for the theatrical stage, have the tendency to get you a bit off line, vocally. Return to your teacher as often as is feasible to get yourself lined up again. Only your teacher can properly fine-tune your voice. You cannot hear yourself as others hear you, and you need this objective control from one who knows your voice well.

Also, when learning a new role, don't just study it with your coach. Run it through with your teacher to find possible vocal snags that need to be removed. That is more a job for the teacher than the coach.

Another bit of advice: after you have carefully chosen your teacher, please give him/her a break. Studying with a new teacher usually produces some instant progress due to a burst of enthusiasm and hope on the part of the pupil. After you have settled into a routine of two or three lessons a week (the minimum necessary for good progress) the initial enthusiasm wears off and old problems do not disappear as quickly as anticipated. You are disappointed to find yourself on a vocal plateau, but that is not cause for immediately switching to another teacher. There is no substitute for persistence and hard work and some stubborn problems require just that. You must give a good teacher six months to a year to produce real results. There is no instant path to success. Unfortunately, some singers are habitual tasters; they never are patient enough to really absorb and digest anything.

When I first began studying with Margolis, I showed some immediate improvement. Within a month, two or three other Met singers, noticing the difference in my singing, came running to my new maestro's studio. Within three months, they had run off to yet another teacher. Now, it was six months before some of my major problems began to yield to good teaching. I remained with Margolis for more than twenty-five years. In contrast to this, I had a baritone friend who bragged that he had studied voice with thirty-nine different teachers. And he was the worst singer I have ever heard.

Let me warn you, though, that no teacher knows it all. My three maestri were all quite good, but, in retrospect, not one of them was perfect. Do not be lured into some sort of Svengali-Trilby relationship. The teacher is not creating you, but should be creating a mutual, working relationship. Naturally, your teacher should know more than you do about singing and you should subject yourself to his/her guidance. But your part in this relationship is to keep an open mind and to be willing to experiment with your vocal apparatus.

Never forget that one of the greatest teachers is the stage itself. Singing in a large hall is an entirely different experience from singing in the studio, and there is no substitute for it. Take every opportunity to set foot on the stage of a large theater. It is a terrible shock for some inexperienced young singers to be suddenly thrust into the real world of giant stages and halls.

The real secret of singing in the big halls is to tease the hall into singing with you. Perhaps I have put that badly. You cannot make a hall do anything: you must adapt to it. You must sing in such a way that you stir up the bathtub-echo effect. Then the hall sings a duet with you and your own natural sound is enhanced and made more beautiful.

Another important way of learning is to listen to live performances, videos and records of great singers. Seek to find what they can do and you can't. When you find some extraordinary singer of your vocal category who can do things that seem unattainable to you, don't brush it off as a freak voice. That would be a cop-out on your part, the way of avoiding a challenge which could be important to your career.

When Joan Sutherland was young, she could not sing above a high B-flat. She could have decided that Maria Callas had a freak voice, and so would have avoided the challenge of trying to compete. She decided, instead, that if Callas could do it, so could she. The word "can't" was not part of her vocabulary. And it should not be part of yours either! Make up your mind right now that "can't" is a four-letter word and should be replaced by "how."

126

Also, consider that you will eventually have to accept the responsibility of teaching yourself to some extent. When you travel worldwide as a professional, you will be on your own; your teacher will not likely be travelling with you. You will confront crisis after crisis that will bring new challenges into your life and no one will be there to guide you.

No matter what your training, when you set foot on that stage, the ultimate responsibility for your success or failure will yours, not your teacher's. The critics will not be there to review your teacher, they will be there to review YOU! The audience, which is the ultimate critic, will not cheer or jeer your maestro, but will only cheer or jeer YOU! If you are successful, well and good. If you fail, there will be no chance to lay the blame on someone else. If you have any guts, you will take your lumps and get up from the mat and come back fighting again.

And, as a final piece of advice, whenever something goes wrong, automatically blame yourself first, even if it eventually turns out not to be the case. Don't allow yourself to fall into the destructive habit of blaming others, or just blind circumstance, for your problems. And there is a good rationale for this: your problem will rarely be someone else's fault, or just bad luck over which you have no control. Rarely are you the innocent victim of circumstance.

Actually, if your problem is self-inflicted and caused by something YOU did wrong, that is good news in disguise. Why? Because it means YOU can do something about it! You are not a helpless victim and have a certain measure of control over the situation.

Always remember that you are never a failure until you blame someone else for your problems. My personal experience has been that 95 percent of my troubles were self-inflicted. As a young singer, I tried to excuse my red, swollen vocal folds by calling myself a "post-nasal drip." I was a "drip" all right, but not "post-nasal." My vocal folds were red and swollen from vocal abuse, not from some low-grade infection or mysterious allergy. I must admit that 5 percent of the time (and only 5 percent) the fault was not mine and I had incorrectly blamed myself. But, being wrong 5 percent of the time is far better than being wrong 95 percent of the time, which would have been the case had I continually laid the blame on everything else.

In conclusion, let me wish you the good fortune of finding the *right teacher*. But, I also wish you the good fortune of finding the *right pupil*, deep down inside YOU!

P.S. I have decided to add a Post Script to this chapter. When I am asked with whom I have studied singing and acting, I generally speak of Gennaro Curci, Rocco Pandiscio and Samuel Margolis as my voice teachers and Vladimir Rosing as my drama coach. But, as I reflect, the truth of the matter is that I should say that I have personally studied voice and drama with "everyone."

When I interviewed forty of my famous colleagues for *Great Singers on Great Singing.* I learned more about vocal technique in three short years than I had learned in my whole life. Also, when a singer would take a few private lessons with me, they didn't realize that I was often learning from them as well. Many times a student comes to study with me and shows some very special ability. I become curious as to what that student is doing so different from everyone else and I try to understand and acquire that special something for myself. In that sense I have studied with everyone.

Perhaps the strangest learning experience I had of drama was when I studied with our toy poodle, Lulu. Lulu was a little eight pound orphan we picked up in a dog grooming shop. She loved my wife, Lucia, with a passion and barely tolerated me. If I did anything to annoy her, she would go after me with a vengeance. In bed at night, if I moved and disturbed her sleep, she would warn me with a nasty growl. If I didn't heed that warning, she would go after my legs under the covers and actually chase me out of bed.

Now, we had two other dogs as well, a larger, well-mannered poodle, Loretta, and a nasty, sixty-five pound mixed breed that had chewed up everybody in the family, the hired help, and the neighbors as well. His name was Boris. It should have been "Ivan the Terrible!" As vicious as he was, he was absolutely terrified of Lulu! When he came through the TV room to go outside, he had to pass Lulu's doggie bed and he knew he was going to get it from her when he tried to sneak by. He would actually climb up on and over a chair by the wall to avoid her ferocious attacks.

It was quite a sight to watch this little drama three or four times a day. As Boris would try to sneak by, Lulu's spine would suddenly coil up and tense like a rattlesnake about to strike, her body frozen in a terrible tension, eyes bugging and fixed on Boris. There she sat, rigid, with bared fangs—until she struck—like lightning!

Now, if you were to watch me in the mad-scene from *Boris Godunov* when I storm at Prince Shuiski, you would see Lulu about to strike as my spine stiffens and coils like a rattlesnake. Yes, I studied *Boris Godunov* with an eight pound toy poodle and she was a mighty good teacher.

Now, I said that I study with everybody, but there is one person that deserves special mention: Lucia Evangelista Hines, my bride of forty-five years, mother of my four sons, but also the toughest and most reliable critic I have ever faced. If she had been a critic for the *New York Times,* I never would have had a career.

But, seriously, she has an incredible ear and knows my voice like no one else. Since Maestro Margolis died, I have let Lucia be the one who approves or disapproves of every sound I make and it has been a most rewarding experience for me. We all need someone with a good ear who truly has our well-being at heart and will not spare us from the truth.

May you be so fortunate as to have someone like her in your life, someone who really cares and can be so painfully honest.

CHAPTER XIV

GENERAL HEALTH

W hat are the most important factors to be considered in
dealing with the human voice? Is it not enough to
choose the right teacher, concentrating primarily on
vocal technique and musical preparation? Naturally, these factors
are of prime importance, but I feel that one of the most basic
issues to address is care of the God-given instrument you have
inherited; for without a healthy voice you might as well forget
about a singing career.

The first thing to remember is that your entire body is related
to the vocal apparatus. What affects any single part of your body
will affect your singing as well. A pain in your foot will detract
from your concentration in performance. An emotional crisis can
actually alter the physical condition of your delicate vocal folds.
Sunburn on the day of a performance can rob the vocal folds of a

much needed blood supply. Eating a steak between acts can provide enough tryptophan to immediately act as a sedative to a hyper-emotional singer. A glass of wine or cognac during the show will immediately cause an edema (swelling and reddening) of the vocal folds, at the same time fooling the gullible singer into believing he or she is singing better (it will seem better to the performer, but definitely not to the audience).

Literally everything that happens to the body affects the voice. So, care of the body is critical for the singer. In this chapter we will concentrate on good health, both physical and mental.

First, is being *fat* conducive to good singing? And if not, why do so many singers claim it to be so? Even though the Surgeon General has never made an issue of it, a singer's lifestyle can be hazardous to his or her health. Generally, a singer eats the main meal of the day rather early. Then, after three or four hours of strenuous performance, the famished artist immediately heads for the nearest beanery for a "midnight snack" of pasta and steak. Following that, one must have at least nine or ten hours of sleep on a full stomach. What better way to accumulate the extra pounds so often associated with successful opera singers?

When the singer's figure begins to get a bit too gross, the crash diet appears. With it come the inevitable consequences of lethargy and weakness, due to an unbalanced nutritional intake—more appropriately described as "malnutrition."

The singer might even try exercise as a last resort. But what commonly happens when unused muscles are called into play? There is stiffness and soreness, and the blood supply is diverted away from the vocal folds to those muscles. When that happens, the voice can get scratchy or heavy. Whatever the side effects, they will not be good. Does that mean exercise is bad for the voice? Hardly! One must work out the initial soreness and stiffness with more exercise. With continuing workouts the vocal folds will receive an ever increasing supply of blood which will eventually be most beneficial for the voice. Unfortunately, a singer who has suffered vocally from the initial exercise often decides that any exercise is bad for the voice and should be avoided.

When one's manager complains about losing contracts to competitors whose singers have inferior voices but better figures, there is often a panicky return to some freaky diet, and one gets into the proverbial "yoyo" routine where the end is worse than the beginning.

What is the solution to this anguishing situation? It is simple: don't think *thin* or *fat* think *HEALTH*. And to quote the late Paul C. Bragg, my health mentor of many years, "Good health is simply a matter of good plumbing." The body has two main sets of plumbing, the circulatory system and the gastrointestinal tract. Keep these two sets of piping open and clean and you will be on the road to good health. And how is that to be accomplished? By approaching "good health" through proper nutrition, exercise and—I hesitate to say it, but I must—FASTING!

While I will attempt to lay down some general rules for these three disciplines, Bragg did it better. I strongly recommend going to health food stores and looking up his booklets on nutrition, exercise and fasting. Since his premature, accidental demise at the early age of ninety-five, his daughter, Patricia Bragg, has been carrying the torch for the cause. His booklets are increasingly difficult to find, but are well worth the trouble.

First let us consider what constitutes proper nutrition. I will not recommend a fad diet, but a nutritional regimen that should ideally be practiced for the rest of your life. You will find no "yoyo" in that.

On a fad diet you temporarily deny yourself all of the goodies that seemingly make mealtime worthwhile. Then after an incredible display of willpower, for a seemingly interminable span of time, you reach the desired weight and the need for such stringent behavior is over. Surely, you can have just one slice of that delicious lemon meringue pie. And there go your weeks, even months, of effort as your willpower collapses like a deflating balloon.

Instead, I would like to suggest that you make up your mind to adopt a health regimen that will ensure you longlasting results.

133

When you give up junk food and go on a healthy diet, you are no longer committed to the goal of a certain number of pounds; you are committed to the goal of a long, vigorous life. Now you can start thinking health instead of fat, since fat is simply not healthy. That means you can only afford to go off this diet the day they bury you, but not before. Okay, no health regimen will make you live forever, but at least when you die you will know it was not from anything serious.

Removing tongue from cheek, let us continue discussing healthful eating. What are the junk foods that we should avoid? Are you ready for this? Here is a partial list:

No-No's
Processed foods
Refined sugar
Refined or bleached flour products
Foods with artificial flavors
Foods with preservatives and chemical additives
Polysaturated fats
Pork products
Salt
Carbonated drinks
Tea and coffee
Tap water and mineral water

At first, you may say, "What is there left to eat?" What, for example, would a raw salad taste like without salt? And cashews, walnuts or peanuts? But let me assure you that a wee bit of creativity can wreak miracles. Yes, I missed salt in my raw salads until Loretta Corelli (Franco's wife) served me one with chopped apple and onion mixed in. It was delicious. And you might also try a salad dressing made of apple cider vinegar, canola oil and a bit of honey.

Let me assure you that after about six months on a salt-free diet, your taste will change. Nuts with salt are now unpleasant to me, and I really used to be a saltaholic. Hang in there, there is hope.

"All right, what," you may ask, "is wrong with mineral water?"

Any water, except "distilled" (which is pure water as it pours down as rain), contains inorganic minerals, which are nothing but different types of salts. These minerals may be essential to the functioning of the human body but not in the inorganic form in which you find them in mineral waters: they cannot be absorbed nutritionally in this inorganic form; they must first be chelated. Chelation provides an organic form of the mineral which can be absorbed and utilized by the body. Unfortunately, your system can only successfully chelate about 6 percent of the organic minerals you imbibe and the rest must either be eliminated through the kidneys or end up deposited in the arteries.

How, then, are our bodies to acquire these chelated minerals which are essential to life if we do not acquire them through our water supply? Actually, the ideal source of chelated minerals is raw fruit and raw vegetables. Almost half of your diet should consist of them. Ideally, vegetable salads should be based upon raw carrot and cabbage along with other crunchy fare such as cauliflower, broccoli, celery and beets.

You will have the choice of going lacto-vegetarian, vegan (vegetarian without dairy products), or of eating chicken, veal, seafood and meats—in moderation. This must be your own personal choice. But what is important is to try to eat things that are natural, however that statement has to be qualified. Some dimwits say, "If it's natural, it can't hurt you." That, of course, is ridiculous. Arsenic is natural. So are strychnine and botulism.

You probably will not want to be such a dietary fanatic as indicated above, and will have to decide just how much health you would like to have.

Now, on to exercise. First of all, it should be a kind of exercise that you can indulge in almost anywhere. The simplest thing would be to walk at least two miles a day. That you can do at home or on tour, in the country or in the city.

135

Aside from walking, I have always been a water nut. I feel as though half of my life has been spent underwater. I began spearfishing in 1942, and scuba diving in 1952. My entire family dives. Although my opera-diva wife, Lucia, did not take up scuba until the age of sixty-two, she has, to date, made 238 dives, and has been as deep as 135 feet on various occasions. She leaves the 200-foot dives to me.

Scuba is a pleasant, invigorating sport that helps keep you in shape. I do not recommend that all opera singers become scuba-divers, but I do recommend swimming as well as walking or jogging. A membership in a health spa is also a good idea, and I think that a vigorous workout is healthful, and good for the voice.

Don't get the mistaken idea that exercise alone is sufficient for good health without any need for proper nutrition. I recall visiting a friend who, at forty-seven, got turned on to jogging and tennis. I warned him to add good nutrition to the list, but he wasn't interested. He explained that he had never smoked or drunk alcoholic beverages in his whole life and that he was building a strong heart with exercise.

I pointed out that having a powerful pump could lead to trouble if the pipes are clogged: enough clogging and something will blow out. Unfortunately, something did blow out a few months later on the tennis court. I had sung at his wedding and then I had to sing at his funeral. I cannot help but feel that more attention to his plumbing, instead of just the pump, could have made a difference.

Lastly, let us discuss the most controversial and, from my experience, the most valuable of all health practices: FASTING—on distilled water.

When I first became a health nut, I began with healthful nutrition, exercise and *fasting one day a week*. After about four months of this routine I tried fasting for two consecutive days. I was surprised to find I was not hungry at all on the morning of the second day. And I was also surprised to find I had more energy on that second day than when I began.

In my tenth month as a health nut, I decided to go four days on distilled water alone. I was amazed to see how easy it was, and then I became curious as to how my singing voice would behave after ninety-six hours without food. I sat at the piano and vocalized for forty-five minutes without stopping. It shocked me to find how clear my voice was and also what excellent stamina I had. I then realized I had just exploded a myth which I had previously defended: that one had to have ample food during the day to maintain the strength to sing.

It was also interesting to note that each day of the fast I seemed to gain energy. There is a reason for that: we burn up a great deal of energy every day digesting the protein in our diet. During a fast that energy becomes available for other things. For example, the diverted energy is useful in fighting disease; which explains why all animals stop eating when they are sick.

Finally, I decided to try a seven-day fast. My best friend was a prominent surgeon in New Jersey, and when he heard I was going to fast for a week on distilled water alone he told my wife to not let me do it, insisting that conclusive medical research had shown this to be dangerous. He and I got into a heated argument about it and I challenged him to dig up that research he was quoting and show it to me. A week later he sheepishly reported he had looked up the research. "Go on and do it," he said, "it won't hurt you."

Since then I have found most doctors to be adamant in their objections to fasting, but totally ignorant of the facts. Several years ago my family doctor found I had considerable liver damage, probably from a case of hepatitis. I informed him that I was going to do a seven day fast to cure the condition and he had a fit.

"You absolutely must not fast at a time like this," he said emphatically. "When the liver is damaged you must feed it protein." I quickly protested, noting how effective fasting was in curing illness. His response was, "That is contrary to all I was taught in medical school. You must feed the liver or it will be further damaged."

I made up my mind then that, as a matter of principle, I had to

137

fast to know the truth. I decided that after the seven day fast we would run another liver scan, and if my condition worsened, I would rethink my opinions on fasting. He warned against it, but I persisted in going on the fast.

After seven days we ran another liver scan. The doctor reluctantly reported to me that my liver had returned completely to normal, and that I now showed an immunity to both A and B Hepatitis. For me fasting has proven to be a most healthful practice.

I now expect your reaction to be: "If I don't eat for a full day I get shaky and develop a headache."

Well, so did I the first time. But that syndrome soon disappeared. The explanation is simple: you get shaky and develop a headache because you are releasing poisons from the toxic junk buried in your fat tissues. Most human beings have a large amount of fat-soluble trash dissolved in their fatty tissues. It basically comes from the environment in the form of pesticides and preservatives in your food, medications, second-hand smoke from tobacco, fumes from auto exhausts, etc.

Now these poisons, buried in your fatty tissue, lie dormant as long as you keep on eating. When you stop eating the body begins to burn its fat reserves for energy and as the fat enters the bloodstream, the toxic poisons come with it. Poisons that have been filtered out and are lingering in the liver are also released into the bloodstream.

It is the accumulated junk your body has stored in its fatty tissue that makes you feel sick when you stop eating. After you have gone through several extended fasts and have cleaned out the fatty tissue, you will no longer get the shakes and headaches. Fasting then becomes a much more pleasant experience.

I would also like to report a most interesting observation regarding cholesterol. We all know that if you suffer from high cholesterol, your doctor will recommend a low cholesterol diet, exercise and various other remedies. After about three or four months the level of cholesterol in your blood may have dropped by twenty points. Well and good.

But I had a strange set of experiences that should give the medical profession some thought. Three times, under medical supervision, I have dropped my cholesterol level forty to fifty points in just seven days. My doctors were astonished, particularly because I did it with a high cholesterol diet. They were astonished but didn't want to discuss it because the AMA has nothing to say about it. I was shocked by their lack of interest.

The diet I am describing has been called "The Air Force Diet," and also "The Low Carbohydrate Diet." On this regimen you eat fifty grams of carbohydrate a day, no more, no less. But you eat as much protein as you want all day, leaning particularly on foods such as eggs, beef, cheese, etc. All of these are high cholesterol items. In one week's time you will have lost five pounds on a constantly full stomach and your cholesterol will have dropped precipitously.

How can that be? It is simple, the demon in high blood cholesterol is not the cholesterol itself, but the carbohydrates. When you have both sugar and fat in the bloodstream, the body will selectively choose to metabolize the sugar and store the fat. In that storing of unused fat, cholesterol (which is of the fat family) is likewise being accumulated instead of being metabolized.

Notice I said you have to have 50 grams of carbohydrate, no more, no less. If you don't have this minimal amount of carbohydrate in your system, you will develop a condition called "ketosis" and your breath will begin to smell like acetone.

I do not say I advocate the diet on a long term basis, as the long term effects are not known. It might be eventually harmful to the kidneys (and indeed those with kidney problems might be wise to avoid it). Your doctor would probably know more about that than you do, but I feel it is a subject worthy of some real scientific investigation.

However fanatical you decide to become about health is up to you. But good health will not only improve your quality of life, but also your quality of singing. Think about it—seriously!

The Problem of Travel

Singers often face a serious situation that does not directly affect the voice, but can be problematic: flying to engagements when one has a cold. With a bacterial infection of the respiratory tract, flying can be quite hazardous because of the serious possibility of incurring an inner ear infection.

After one such bad experience in the early eighties, I asked my doctor when the stuffy feeling in my ears would subside and my hearing would return to normal. His prognosis shocked me:

"Your hearing will not return to normal," he said and his prediction was accurate. As a result of two more inner ear infections soon after, I was left with distinctly impaired hearing; since then I have been forced to resort to hearing aids.

Believe me, it is not easy to adjust to singing with such a serious handicap, but it can be done. However, please take my advice and do not fly with a respiratory infection, even if it means losing an engagement.

Another hazard to take seriously is jetlag due to a change in time zones. A two or three hour time change is not too serious, but changes of six to twelve hours can be deadly. I am sure we are all different, but when I personally face such a large change, I find it takes me a minimum of seven days to adjust, particularly if I am flying from West to East.

The worst challenge of this sort I ever faced was in the early eighties when I commuted between Rome, Italy, where I was rehearsing and performing *Pelléas and Mélisande* and other engagements on the Metropolitan Opera tour. I made four round trips from Rome to places such as Toronto and Cleveland in one month. I hope you will never be so silly as to emulate this kind of behavior— I swear I will not try it again.

For the first time in my life, I resorted to taking sleeping pills the moment I got on each of those trans-Atlantic flights. At that time Halcion was a new drug and its side effects were not yet well established. On my third trip to Rome, I arrived in a stupor at 8:30 a.m. and

140

went directly to the theater for a 10:00 a.m. dress rehearsal. I dosed myself with some strong caffé espresso and went right on stage. That afternoon I returned to our apartment and collapsed in bed.

I was one of the first people to experience the drastic side effects of Halcion. For the next twelve hours I found myself in a panic and was convinced I was on the verge of dying. I have always been very stable emotionally and it was a weird experience that gave me some all too realistic insight as to what a nervous breakdown feels like. I do not intend to ever go through anything like that again.

So, heed my advice and stay away from unnatural manipulation of the body through drugs whenever possible. And be wiser than I; do not bite off more than you can chew!

CHAPTER XV

VOCAL HEALTH AND TRAUMA

L et us now discuss the various types of vocal trauma that a
singer can encounter during a long career.

Broken Blood Vessels

"You have a broken blood vessel on the right vocal cord and you
won't sing for three months," was the doctor's gloomy diagnosis. I
had a recital in Columbus, Ohio and within a few moments of going
on stage I was suddenly unable to even speak. After folding up in my
first number, I made my excuses to the audience and went backstage
to ask if there were a throat specialist in the house. A doctor was
quickly found and he happened to have his medical bag in his car.

His prognosis of a three-month recovery was devastating
because I was to make my debut at La Scala, Milan in about five
weeks. And how permanent would the damage be? In fact, the word

quickly began to circulate around Columbus that I was "finished" and it soon spread as far as New York.

I returned to New Jersey completely stunned and went directly to Dr. Leo Reckford's office. I faced my visit with great dread: a broken blood vessel on a vocal cord sounded so ominous. It was something singers just didn't talk about. There were those dramatic stories about how Enrico Caruso coughed up blood on the Metropolitan Opera stage from just such a trauma. Wasn't that what killed him? (Of course not! He died months later in Italy of a pleural infection, but that doesn't sound as dramatic as the popular Hollywood movie version.)

Dr. Reckford took one look at my vocal folds (as we now call them) and said, "Yes, a broken vessel on the right cord. You won't sing for six days."

"Six days? The other doctor said three months."

"Well, he's wrong. You will be fine in a week."

He then explained that a broken blood vessel is a minor thing if it is not on the edge of the cord. Singing with a broken vessel on the edge of the cord could scar it permanently, which would be very serious. But a broken vessel in the middle of the cord has no lasting consequences. I asked him how common this sort of trauma was among singers. He said roughly 50 percent of all professionals have it at least once during their careers and that some are more prone to it than others because of fragile capillaries.

He went on to say that it was not the result of the way one sang, but was caused by a sudden burst of blood pressure from a cough or a sneeze. In other words, it did not mean the artist was singing wrong. All this was very comforting and I am glad to report that I had no trouble carrying out my assignment the next month in Milano.

Because of this incident, I came to realize that singers should freely discuss their vocal traumas since it would save a great deal of panic when some unusual condition such as this occurs. How many singers do you know that would admit having had this kind of problem? Probably none because they are afraid it will brand them as being poor singers.

Altogether, I have had this trauma occur three times in fifty-four years of singing. The second time, I was performing at Lake Chautauqua. The day before my final performance of Don Quixote in *Man of La Mancha*. I was at a dinner party when it happened. In a matter of minutes I could barely speak. No, I had not sung at all that day, but I have been prone to an elevated blood pressure since I had scarlet fever at the age of twenty-two.

I went to my hotel room and took a look at my vocal cords and, sure enough, the right cord was the scarlet color associated with this condition. The break was clearly in the middle of the left cord.

I called to Dr. Reckford in New York and explained the situation.

"Is it on the edge of the cord?" he asked.

I told him it was not, so he asked me what I had to sing. I told him it was one performance of *La Mancha*.

"In what key do you do 'The Impossible Dream?'"

When I told him A-flat, he said, "Then your highest note will only be D-flat. You can do it. You will sound terrible, but at least you can save the show (I had no understudy). Go ahead, you won't hurt yourself. And come and see me the day you get back."

So, after an announcement of indisposition to the audience, I sang—and badly—but no harm was done. In fact, I performed two consecutive outdoor concerts with the Detroit Symphony two weeks later with no ill effects. And those tough concerts included excerpts from *Die Walküre* and *Boris Godunov*.

One last observation regarding this sort of trauma. Dr. Reckford always maintained that broken blood vessels on the vocal folds were not the result of singing incorrectly. He always insisted that it was the result of a sudden burst of blood pressure, such as a sneeze or a cough.

At first, I did not buy this. Then the occasion arose in which a popped blood vessel was found on my left vocal fold. However, it had not broken. Dr. Anthony Jahn, my laryngologist since

145

Reckford's death, was sure that it was not going to go away by itself and suggested that I consider having it removed surgically.

The problem was that I was contracted to do three Wagner concerts that week in Baltimore in which I had to sing "Wotan's Farewell," a very challenging piece for me. I was worried that the strain of doing such heroic singing, with its high tessitura, might cause the vessel to break during the performance, yet I decided to go through with the concerts and have the surgery afterwards. Needless to say, I approached the performances with great apprehension. I hoped and prayed that Dr. Reckford was right about the true cause of this sort of trauma. And, to my pleasant surprise, I successfully performed the three concerts without any sudden vocal collapse.

Immediately afterwards, I returned home to New Jersey. The next morning I awoke to the tail end of a heavy snow storm, got out a snow shovel and went to work. After ten minutes of heavy exertion I returned to the house, and when I tried to speak to my wife, I found myself completely voiceless. Suspecting what had happened, I ran into the bathroom to look at my vocal folds. Sure enough, the left fold was vermilion. After the trauma subsided, a visit to Dr. Jahn disclosed that there was no evidence of the original problem.

This was a dramatic confirmation of Dr. Reckford's claim that singing was not the cause of this trauma, but that it was the result of a sudden rise in blood pressure, such as I had incurred by shoveling snow.

Seeing Your Own Vocal Folds

Being able to see your own vocal folds is very important, since they behave better if they know you are watching them. But, seriously, what I am about to write here will be of particular importance if you find yourself in bad voice in a strange locality that does not have a laryngologist who is highly experienced in treating opera singers. Seeing one's vocal folds is easily accomplished by buying a dental mirror at the pharmacy and attaching it to a pencil flashlight, as in the following diagram:

146

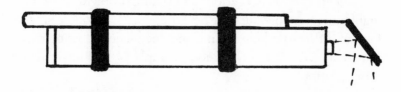

In the bathroom, face the wall mirror with the lights off. Hold the dental mirror under the hot water tap for a few moments, quickly wipe it free of hot water with a handkerchief and then, looking closely into the wall mirror, use the handkerchief to pull your tongue out and insert the dental mirror/flashlight into your mouth, with the dental mirror going back past the uvula and reflecting down so you can see your vocal folds.

This should enable you to see if your vocal folds are smooth, straight and white. Should there be any irregularity on one or both of the folds, rest the voice until the folds are smooth. The same is to be recommended if there is pinkness on the folds or if one fold seems to be wider than the other. But, in case of any irregularity, see an experienced laryngologist as soon as possible.

If the folds are pink or red, do not fall into the trap of saying you have a post-nasal drip. Accept the fact that you are probably abusing your voice by singing too much, or incorrectly. The same will hold true if one fold is distinctly wider looking than the other—that is a swollen vocal fold and it calls for vocal rest.

If there is a bulge on a vocal fold or any rough irregularity, that is also due to a self-inflicted trauma and requires vocal rest.

In the case of a very sudden loss of voice, namely in a matter of half a minute, suspect a broken blood vessel. When seen in the laryngeal mirror, the afflicted vocal fold will be vermilion and swollen. The center of the break will be distinguishable, and if it is on or near the edge of the vocal fold, do not touch your voice until you have seen a specialist. Otherwise the damage you will inflict in trying to sing over it can be permanent.

147

Nodes

We singers have a very serious and vexing problem: most local laryngologists have had little or no experience with opera singers and are of little or no help in an emergency. The following experience I had will give you a good example of this unfortunate kind of situation.

How often has some particular teacher claimed to be able to cure nodes without surgery by proper vocal therapy. I, personally, do not believe this to be realistic and here is why: I have been told at least twice during my career that I had nodes, but it was a false alarm in both cases.

For example, I was down South rehearsing Mephistopheles in *Faust* while fighting a windpipe infection. My voice responded fairly well until the first orchestra rehearsal and by the day of the dress I was obviously in trouble.

I was sent to the "number one" laryngologist of this major city (he shall mercifully remain nameless) who, after examining me, said that I had nodes. NODES, the anathema for all singers? Well, I fortunately knew better than to listen to him.

"Doctor," I said, patronizingly, "I did not have nodes five days ago and it takes at least six months to produce nodes."

"I'm sorry, but I'm telling you what I see," he stated emphatically. He then proceeded to draw me a sketch of the typical twin peaks that he saw on my vocal folds. Yep, they sure looked liked nodes! But I knew better. I then asked him if I might use his telephone, and called Dr. Reckford in New York. After I explained the situation, Dr. Reckford asked to speak to the laryngologist. After an involved discussion the doctor handed the phone back to me. Reckford said, "Get out of there as fast as you can. Try to get an ultrasonic on your larynx somewhere, but it probably won't be of too much help. When you get back to town, come in and I'll take care of you. It won't be very serious."

Well, I was not able to sing the performances, but when I got back to New York the so-called nodes were gone, and I was soon back to performing without surgery and without the help of some so-called therapist who claimed to "cure nodes without it." The trouble is that a doctor who has had no experience with professional opera singers has no idea of the seemingly devastating looking damage a singer can inflict on the vocal folds in a very short time. But that damage, when properly handled, can usually be reversed just as quickly.

So, the next time you hear that you have nodes, don't be in such a great hurry to run to the surgeon's scalpel. If the condition has arisen quickly, it will most likely go away just as quickly.

The Common Cold

One day after I had a treatment by Dr. Reckford, he opened a large closet that had four shelves crammed full of bottles of all sizes and shapes. Seeing my quizzical look, he said, with a chuckle, "All this to fight the common cold! If we had a cure, there would only be one bottle."

Every time I came down with a cold before a performance, some well meaning expert would suggest some homespun remedy. Over the years, I dutifully tried many of them, without much positive result. Yes, I chewed garlic cloves, swallowed thousands of grams of vitamin C, faithfully took my cod-liver oil—you name it.

The common medical treatment for a cold is to first take an antibiotic during the rhinitis stage. This has no effect on the viral infection which is causing your runny nose, but is often effective in preventing a secondary bacterial infection. The next step is to take a derivative of cortisone, such as prednisone, as soon as you are sure all of the infection is gone. This is to reduce any edema, or swelling, from the mucous tissues. You must be careful that the infection has completely left your system before taking the steroid, or the infection will tend to return and spread.

In 1972, I had a serious windpipe infection and was desperate to recover quickly because I had a six-week tour ahead. I was treated, treated and treated again, constantly trying to keep from cancelling performances. As hard as I fought to recover, I kept relapsing, and went on like this for the entire month and a half. I finally returned home and paid a visit to Dr. Reckford.

"This is out of my hands now," he said. "Go see your physician, you have pneumonia." That was a shock! I was due to start rehearsing *Faust* in a week. I returned home and consulted my surgeon friend, Dr. Arthur D'Alessandro. After confirming the diagnosis, he asked me what medications I was taking. I gave him a considerable list and he told me to drop them all.

"Go to bed for a week and stay on a juice diet. No food for one week and you'll be all right." I did as told and was able to do the *Faust*, but I was tired of these prolonged, relapsing illnesses that seem to so commonly plague us opera singers.

I called Patricia Bragg, the daughter of Paul C. Bragg, the dean of American health nuts, and asked her how I could avoid problems like this in the future. She called her father in Hawaii and he sent me the following advice: Go to bed and fast on nothing but distilled water until the cold is gone. I have followed this advice ever since and no cold has ever lasted longer than two or three days. The remedy is simple, but effective.

What about the old adage, "Feed a cold and starve a fever?" Probably the original meaning of this was "If you feed a cold, you will have to starve a fever." So do as your pet dog or cat would do— when you are sick, stop eating—fast! But we spoke about that in Chapter XIV in our discussion on health.

However, I do have a somewhat positive report to give on a more recent experience. Two years ago, Eileen Strempel, one of our OMTI protégés, said she had been taking the herb *echinacea* for three years and had not had a single cold. It has been claimed that this natural herb stimulates the immune system. So, I began taking two capsules every day, which is not the recommended dosage and procedure, but it seemed to be highly effective. I had only one minor cold in two years (and that because I forgot to take my *echinacea*). What a miracle it has been for me, since, from childhood, I have been prone to contracting more than my share of colds.

The Lump You Can't Swallow

Most singers have at one time experienced the strange feeling of having a lump in the throat (actually in the laryngeal region) that won't go down when they swallow. It is commonly associated with a sensation of muscular tension on one side of the larynx. This is the result of pinching the laryngeal nerve by overdoing it when trying to pull the voice up high in the mask. It is sometimes accompanied by a pulling of the mouth to one side when singing—actually the side on which the muscular ache is felt.

The immediate symptom of the "lump you can't swallow" can be effectively eliminated by a procedure discovered by the late Dr. Leo P. Reckford. It consists of an intravenous injection of calcium gluconate. This chelated form of calcium is most effective in relaxing tense muscles.

But there is a real need to treat the cause of the problem, not just the symptom. I experienced this problem in my early years at the Met, when I was struggling to find good high notes with the false idea that they were "high" and had to be pulled up tightly into the mask. I began getting muscle cramps on the right-hand side of my larynx and, in my early performances with the "Voice of Firestone" telecasts, I was obviously twisting my mouth to the right-hand side. When I got rid of this false premise that high notes were high, I also got rid of this syndrome of the pinched laryngeal nerve and facial contortion, and it has never returned.

In fact, the next time you need a good relaxing sleep, do not just try the naturopath's much-touted dolomite, but take chelated dolomite (an organic form of natural calcium—essentially "chalk") for a really strong result.

Swollen Vocal Folds

Very often a singer is required to perform under less than perfect conditions, but the show must go on! Many times you will be called upon to sing when your vocal folds are reddish and swollen. A quick remedy is to try using a vaso-constrictor (such as Neo-Synephrine) administered directly on the vocal folds. Within seconds, the swelling shrinks noticeably and the voice is much clearer.

The Neo-Synephrine can be administered by dropping it on your vocal folds with an eyedropper. Or you can put some of it under the front of your tongue and suck in your breath, spraying it down into your throat.

I have found two troublesome side effects. At one point I developed a rebound using the Neo-Synephrine and was unable to sing at all for about a half an hour. I avoid this problem by taking 12-Hour Neo-Synephrine about four hours before I have to sing.

When performing *Man of La Mancha* at The Paper Mill Playhouse in New Jersey, I developed elevated blood pressure. My doctor suspected it was being caused by my continual applications of the Neo-Synephrine and he switched me to another vaso-constrictor, Otrovin.

Such self-treatment should only be used in emergency situations and one should be careful to not develop a dependence upon any drug whatsoever.

A very common remedy for swollen vocal folds is the steroid prednisone. This medication is very effective in reducing swelling and inflammation on the vocal folds and, unfortunately, many singers pop it like candy. However, it has many serious side effects, a few of which are stomach ulcers, osteoporosis, edema, cataracts and mental aberrations. It is a drug to be used only under a doctor's orders. And it must never be used when there is an infection present in the body, since it will tend to make it spread.

There is also the very real problem of needing emergency surgery and, if the doctor does not know you are on prednisone, you could die of shock during the operation.

All that behind us, I would like to suggest that if you must use prednisone, it is better to apply it directly to the vocal folds. Crush the tablet into a powder and add a couple of drops of almond oil, also known as "sweet oil." Using a syringe, this can be dropped directly on the vocal folds as follows: a) first, pull out your tongue with a handkerchief, b) touch the syringe gently against the back wall of your throat, c) draw the syringe back a tiny bit and drop the medication directly on the vocal folds.

This will be far more effective than taking the medication orally and can be made even more so by an ultrasonic treatment on the larynx. For more information on using ultrasound, see the chapter on Dr. Leo P. Reckford in *Great Singers on Great Singing*.

It is a shame that opera singers on tour must rely so heavily on self-medication and self-treatment, but the fact is that most medical specialists have little or no experience in treating opera singers and their rather unique problems.

Good luck!

Chapter XVI

Preservation of the Mature Voice

For the last twenty years I have been singing through what is usually considered "the retirement age," and you can bet I have more than carefully studied my many aging colleagues, most of whom have either fallen by the wayside, or into the grave. Now, I am about to make an observation that will contradict what everyone *knows* to be true. And just what is this controversial observation?

Regarding longevity, I have a severe handicap that the vast majority of men will never have to face: I'm a bass.

"What? Why, everyone knows that the bass voice is the last to go. Right?"

WRONG! Examine the record. Ezio Pinza left opera at a reputed fifty-four (actually fifty-seven), and just about every other great bass of history has folded at least in his early sixties.

Then, consider the tenors. Lauritz Melchior was fired from the

Met by Rudolph Bing for insubordination at the age of sixty-seven. Kurt Baum sang his last Radames with the Met at the age of sixty-nine. Jan Peerce sang at the Met with me as Alvaro in *La Forza del Destino* at the age of sixty-five and continued doing concerts well into his late seventies. I heard Giovanni Martinelli sing a good Canio in the Hollywood Bowl at sixty-eight. Richard Tucker and Beniamino Gigli both succumbed to heart attacks in their mid-sixties, and were still singing extremely well. Bassos come nowhere near such a record.

Then why does everyone believe just the opposite? The answer is quite simple. When I was singing at the Met in my late twenties, I would often be met by strangers with, "You are Jerome Hines? Oh, I thought you were much older."

Why did everyone assume I was much older? Because they never saw me on the opera stage without a long white beard and stoop-shoulders. If they weren't seeing a ninety-two-year-old Grand Inquisitor, it was a one-hundred-two-year-old Arkel, or an octogenarian Gurnemanz. Basses start out looking so old that they appear to last forever.

The paradox is that when a basso begins his career, he is too young for the parts he plays. When he is as old as the character he is portraying, he is too old to sing. Catch-22? You'd better believe it.

In the light of cold reason, it is even more surprising that I am still going strong in my mid-seventies. I will now try to share with you some of the various factors I believe have contributed to making me the longest reigning leading singer in the history of the Met, and to having a career that spans five and a half decades.

The first and most important factor in my maintaining such a long career and such vocal condition has been my deep and abiding Christian faith and the assurance that I am doing just what the good Lord wants me to be doing.

The second important factor has been *not* accepting all vocal problems as being the result of age. Naturally, every human voice must eventually age, but most of the problems encountered by the mature singer are not—and I repeat—*not* caused by age. After the age of fifty, "age" becomes the excuse for most of a singer's problems. Actually, the real problem is the singer's ego. Consider the following example:

Say you are one of the greatest tenors of the century. Then a vocal difficulty appears: you begin to lose your high notes. Do you do what a young singer would do? Do you say "I'm off track" or "I need a new teacher?" Oh, no! You will probably say "What do you mean, I'm singing wrong? Don't you know who you are talking to? Don't you know I am the greatest tenor ever? How could I be singing wrong?"

Thus far, I have successfully staved off many of the problems common to mature and aging singers by anticipating how voices deteriorate and seeking solutions before it is too late. For example, one of the common symptoms of deterioration is the wobble.

I am sure that one of the great contributing factors to the wobble is general physical deterioration. There is a tendency to put on weight as one ages. Add to that the fact that many successful singers are already overweight during their peak singing years and the inevitable result is excessive obesity. Muscle turns to fat, and the strength needed to sing properly is no longer available. Without disciplined and controlled use of proper strength, one resorts to force. But what constitutes disciplined use of strength?

For me, disciplined use of strength means having a rigorous system of vocal exercises that one practices faithfully on a regular basis all of one's vocal life. Too many singers have a much more haphazard approach to maintaining the voice. They get up in the morning and try a few notes, then sing a few phrases from an aria or song. It is a bit of this, or a bit of that, but no two days in a row are alike.

Then, as one's strength is slowly depleted, the singer begins to get smart and conserve. The singer "wises up" and sings on the "interest," not the "capital." This supposed "conservation of energy" eventually includes not vocalizing on the day of a performance, which literally entails warming up on the stage during the performance.

As an older singer finds fewer engagements, there is also less incentive to maintain vocal muscle tone by a regular regimen of singing. All of this leads to the wobble that is so typical of the aging singer.

I believe I have avoided the problem of the wobble by taking proper care of the body, of which the vocal instrument is an integral part.

But the wobble is not the only problem facing the aging singer. A more common symptom is a slow loss of the middle and low voices. I have heard various famous singers, both male and female, who, in their early sixties, have a middle voice that sounds like a bag full of broken glass, yet can still toss off heroic high notes that younger singers cannot match. This is a very common form of deterioration. But, we have already discussed this in depth in Chapter VII. Go back and read it again.

One of the most practical pieces of advice I ever received was to come back fighting harder every time you get knocked down. Do not ever succumb to depression and disappointment. Now, I have a certain peculiarity: a great intolerance for such unproductive moods.

Sometimes I find myself unable to sleep at three or four in the morning, feeling some deep emotional turmoil. I hate such feelings, and get out of bed immediately; taking my Bible with me, I go into the kitchen and have it out with the good Lord. First, I thank Him for the situation He has put me in and try to find the blessing that is buried in every problem. According to Romans 8:28, "All things work together for those that love God and are the called according to His purpose." I trust this scripture and try to find the blessing hidden in every challenge.

Well, it serves to keep my life on an even keel, and whether you share my belief or not, you had better find what will serve you as well.

Since there is no profit in feeling sorry for yourself, shape up and determine to always make lemonade when you get a lemon and—if you are having a hard time with the wolf at the door—learn to eat "wolfburgers."

CHAPTER XVII

STAGE FRIGHT

"Stage fright" is a universal problem touching just about all singers and is not necessarily the result of being in bad voice. It is a natural phenomenon and one should not expect it to go away with years of experience on the stage.

Gina Bachauer once told me how she had returned to Paris for some study with her teacher, a famous pianist who had always suffered notoriously from stage fright. He mentioned that an eighteen-year old pianist was making his debut at the Paris Opera House that evening and suggested they go hear him.

After the concert, the Maestro said, "This boy has talent. Let us go backstage and encourage him." When they met him in the dressing room, the Maestro greeted him with, "My, what a difficult assignment for so young a man! You must have been terribly nervous," to which the youngster casually replied, "Me, nervous?

159

What for?" The Maestro's face froze. And then he added, "Don't worry, you have the talent. The nerves will come!"

There are certain parallels between performers on the stage and soldiers in combat. When soldiers are about to go into battle, it is natural for them to fear for their lives: only a psychopath would feel no fear. The soldier's challenge is not to banish fear, but to fight the good fight in spite of it.

The singer must likewise learn to live with stage fright and even learn to utilize it as a positive factor in performance. So, do not expect to lose your stage fright with artistic maturity; in fact, it might prove to be detrimental if you were able to do so.

There is a common blood pressure medication which has been used as a remedy for stage fright. I knew a violinist who began taking this drug before performances, but she soon discovered that the result was disastrous: her nerves completely disappeared, leaving her feeling like a zombie with absolutely no desire to perform.

We all experience a diminution of nervous tension after an exciting and successful opening night when the second performance is faced much more calmly—perhaps too calmly—the opening-night-jitters are gone. That is where trouble can start. With such a low level of nervous energy, you feel as though you were walking in mud. Oh, what you would give for a bit of the nerves that impelled you on opening night!

At the age of twenty-four, I had just received my first Metropolitan Opera contract and was also offered a contract with the Central City Opera in Colorado to perform the role of Osmin in Mozart's *The Abduction from the Seraglio* with Eleanor Steber singing the role of Costanza. For several years, Frank Saint Leger, assistant director of the Met, used the Central City Opera for trying out soloists who would be performing with the Johnson administration the next season in New York City in much of the same repertoire.

On the afternoon of the opening performance, I came to the theatre quite early to do a rather complex makeup. The main stage was dark and as I was groping my way across to go to my dressing room, I suddenly realized that someone was standing silently in front of me facing the empty house. As I drew close, I discovered it was our star of the show, Eleanor Steber.

Eleanor turned to me and collapsed weeping on my shoulder. "Oh, Jerry," she said, "I'm so scared. I used to have such easy high notes, but I couldn't sing soft. Now I've learned to sing piano and I've lost my high voice. I can't sing this role, Jerry, I can't." She broke down into sobs again.

So, here was I, the green kid trying to console the superstar. I did not know what on earth to say, and carried it off the best I could. I knew we all faced tremendous odds with the high altitude of 8,700 feet and fourteen performances back-to-back, and was somewhat intimidated myself. But my role, no matter how challenging, was nothing compared to the difficulty of the role of Costanza.

Eleanor began the first performances with some obvious struggling and then we heard that her parents were coming to hear her. She immediately came down with a bad cold, but sang anyway. That was the first night that her struggles paid off and she began, in spite of the odds, to conquer the role. By the end of the run, she had mastered it and went on the Met stage the next season to a well-earned success. It was through this experience that I began to perceive the steel spine in this remarkable artist.

It was years later, in a Met broadcast of another Mozart opera, that I saw the steel in that remarkable woman again. They had forgotten to page Eleanor to come on stage for her big aria, and I saw the assistant stage manager frantically dragging Eleanor into the wings, just barely in time to enter and sing. She was justifiably upset and again in tears. It was an experience to watch her straighten up, stride on the stage and deliver a glorious performance for Texaco's millions. *There* was an artist who knew how to handle the ever-present nerves that have destroyed so many others.

Franco Corelli, who has been rightfully acclaimed "The Greatest Tenor of the Century," always came through victorious even though he was reputed to be one of the most nervous singers alive. So many people foolishly said his problem was psychological, but they could not have been further from the truth. First of all, he achieved what others could not even hope to do, but to accomplish this, he had to mercilessly push himself and his voice beyond all normal limits.

He once complained to me that he went through hell every time he sang. I pointed out that he delivered the greatest performances of any tenor in the world and had to expect to pay the price for it.

"Think of the man who wanted to be the first to climb Mount Everest," I said. "He knew and accepted the fact that he would have to go through hell to accomplish it. If his goal hadn't been so impossibly hard, everybody would have been up there waiting for him up when he arrived. So don't complain."

On a couple of occasions I sang with Franco when he was not in the best of voice, as happens to all soloists. But in each case, what he began, he finished—and finished gloriously! Here was an artist who was a living dynamo of nervous energy, but also a transformer of that energy into powerful, dynamic expression. He instinctively directed that terrible nervous energy to flow into his voice, eyes, hands and feet, and ended up with a triumph every time. Yes, he was nervous and he did a masterful job of making his nerves serve his entire body in performance.

Most of us make one common mistake. Before and during performances, we follow the standard routine of trying to convince ourselves that we are calm and peaceful when we simply are not! By trying to impose a false sense of calm upon our psyches, we only manage to paralyze ourselves into immobility.

Now that you know Franco's secret, employ it! Never deny your nerves. Use them to the fullest and thank God for them. When you are not nervous, you are really in trouble.

Panic with Conviction

Now let us consider a rare type of crisis that goes beyond the relatively simple problem of stage fright and requires a more

162

extreme solution. If "Panic with Conviction" sounds like a weird statement to make in a book on career technique, believe me, I am not just trying to get your attention with silly talk. Rare occasions crop up in which even the best technique will be of absolutely no use. When and if you find yourself in such a situation, you should know there is pay dirt in "panic" and I will now try to prove it.

Many years ago, the late John Campbell, editor of *Analog Science Fiction,* and the undisputed father of modern science fiction, wrote an intriguing editorial on the importance of panic. He noted that, since all higher forms of life have built-in panic buttons, panic must have a certain survival value or nature would not have so universally provided it. If, then, panic is of importance to survival, when and how can it be of possible use to an opera singer?

Suppose you are scheduled to perform a major role, are seriously indisposed with no understudy and if you do not sing the performance will be cancelled. Somehow you manage to begin the show but your voice progressively worsens to the point that everything you have ever been taught fails you. Then what do you do? I can recall several such occasions during my career, when I had to choose to throw in the towel, or throw everything I knew to the winds and push the panic button!

There were times early in my career when I was in such a panic over being in bad voice for an important assignment that I would find myself actually wishing the theater would burn down. Or, I would walk on the stage where some chorister was probably thinking, "Oh, if only I could be singing that role instead of him." And what was going on in my mind?

"Oh, if only I could hide in the chorus tonight!"

For me, the most frightening of all those occasions took place in Moscow, where I was scheduled to debut in the title role of *Boris Godunov.* I arrived in Russia with a severe windpipe infection. Following the dress rehearsal, the company doctor examined me, and then called the general manager to cancel my appearance. I immediately went to the general manager's office and insisted that I be allowed to sing.

I was informed that at the Bolshoi the company doctor always made the decision whether or not a soloist was in condition to sing. This single performance of "Boris" had been restored to the repertoire specifically for me and there was no way for it to be postponed. Relenting, the general manager made an exception in my case and let me make the final decision, but sternly warned me that I would have no understudy and if I were unable to do the performance it would be cancelled.

The next day I decided to sing, but on the morning of the performance, I was totally laryngitic. I did muster enough voice to begin the performance, but by the time of the crucial finale with its famous death scene, I was unable to even speak my own name.

What a terrible moment it was for me, the climax of two solid years of preparation for the most important performance of my entire career—and now everything was falling apart! Every time I set my foot on the stage, there was the clicking of cameras from the Russian press and the *New York Times* chronicling my performance as the first native-born American to ever perform the title role of *Boris Godunov* at the Bolshoi.

When my entrance came, I plunged onto the stage like a wounded soldier on a battlefield, desperately fighting for his life. Every note I sang felt like my last. Believe me, panic reigned supreme! In those moments of struggle, it never occurred to me that I was portraying a dying man. Then, after what seemed an eternity, I gasped out my last words and crashed precipitously down the stairs. The Bolshoi public broke their tradition of silence throughout the somber finale and leaped screaming to their feet in a standing ovation. I hardly heard it, I was in such a state of shock!

Then I faced my toughest critic, Lucia, who greeted me backstage, weeping her eyes out, saying between sobs that she had never seen me deliver such a powerful and poignant death scene.

Well, if that is the meaning of "Panic With Conviction," then I am in favor of it. I would not care to have to call upon it too often, but it is good to know that your subconscious mind can take over in emergencies and provide almost supernatural strength and know-how. However, do not make a habit of it, or chances are your career will never get off the ground.

Chapter XVIII

The Conductor and Coach

The present generation of conductors is quite different from that of the past. I suppose part of the problem lies in the "Age of Specialization" in which we presently live. The great conductors of the earlier part of this century were a combination of "conductor *and* coach" and soloists faced them much earlier in the preparatory stages of a production than they do today.

It is now customary for coaches to train the singers, then there is usually one ensemble rehearsal with the conductor, devoted to essential fine tuning, immediately followed by the orchestra rehearsals. The basic molding of the singer's interpretation is left almost exclusively to the coaches.

Back in the fifties, I was assigned to sing the role of Sarastro in Mozart's *The Magic Flute* under the baton of Bruno Walter. After he and I had met several times for solo coaching rehearsals, he decided that there simply were not enough working hours in the Met's daily schedule to do the job properly, so he had me come to his apartment in the evenings to further pursue our work. Like all great conductors of that era, Bruno Walter put his personal stamp on each of his soloists.

In ensemble rehearsals it was not uncommon for the conductor to spend a quarter of an hour on just one page of music to capture the fine nuances that he required of us. These painstaking maestros knew every note and word in the score intimately and had very strong opinions as to how they should be used. This was standard procedure when you worked with people such as Fritz Busch, Fausto Cleva, Emil Cooper, Hans Knappertsbusch, Erich Leinsdorf, Georg Solti, Fritz Stiedry, George Szell and Arturo Toscanini.

Since conductors come in all shapes, sizes and temperaments, it is hard to pin down any particular traits that describe the great ones. They all possess basic skills and depth of knowledge in music, but they must also have a very special ability to attract and hold the performer's focused attention in performance. The first anguished cry one hears from the ineffective conductor is, "NOBODY IS WATCHING ME!" That is a sure sign there is not much worth watching!

The great conductors I have worked with have all seemed to have some unique, magnetic quality that made you submit to their authority. And that quality drastically differs in form from one conductor to another. With some, your attention is riveted through fear and intimidation, while with others it is captivated through deep respect. Whatever the approach, the final result is your undivided attention—or you are in for big trouble.

Emil Cooper, leading conductor of the Maryinski Theatre of St. Petersburg, together with Feodor Chaliapin, first brought *Boris Godunov* out of the Soviet Union. When I worked with him at the Old Met, I found he had a unique way of keeping the singer's attention in performance. If he felt you were not watching him, he would abruptly change the tempo and when you desperately looked for him to pull you out of trouble, he would bury himself in the score and let you sink or swim on your own. This may seem to be a drastic method of holding your attention, but believe me it worked—and I know from firsthand experience.

Fausto Cleva was one of the finest Italian conductors with whom I have ever had the opportunity to work. But what a temper! When he was general manager of the Cincinnati Zoo Opera, the leading newspaper actually did a feature story on him entitled "The Terrible Tempered Mr. Bang." His tantrums were legendary, but they were motivated by a deep, almost fanatical devotion to the music. He literally conducted with tears in his eyes and any slight distraction would ignite a firestorm of frustration and anger.

In a performance of *Faust* at the Met, I apparently entered too loudly in the second act quartet after being sternly warned not to. Fausto threw down his baton and cussed me out—right there in performance as we continued singing—only to resume conducting at the next fermata. But I could forgive that man anything simply because I knew his uncontrollable emotions stemmed from a sincere desire to serve the music he adored.

I worked with Cleva for years and received nothing but harsh criticism—to the point where I thought the man hated me. Then came a very special occasion: the last music to be heard on the stage of the Old Met was the final trio from *Faust*. Nicolai Gedda, Marcella Tucci and I were the soloists and Fausto was the conductor. He and I were both seated upstairs in the green room in a sad, nostalgic mood as we waited for our trio to bring down the final curtain on that grand old house—that noble, historic edifice which was about to be trashed by the iron will of Sir Rudolf.

In a moment of temporary insanity, I declared to the feisty Maestro that he was my favorite Italian conductor (which he was) and, to my shock, he said, "And you are my favorite basso." All those years I had assumed he so intensely disliked me... Yes, conductors come in all shapes, sizes and temperaments—and, believe me, I miss my "Terrible Tempered Mr. Bang." I really do.

Physical appearance, especially impressive size, can serve to intimidate one into respect but it is not, by any means, the important factor. Arturo Toscanini was a man short of stature, as were Fausto Cleva, Pierre Monteux, Anton Coppola, Eugene Ormandy, et al. And don't think for a moment that they were unaware of it. When I performed and recorded the Brahms *Requiem* with Ormandy at the Mormon Tabernacle in Salt Lake City, he made an unusual request:

"Jerome," he said, "since you are a very religious man and I am a very little man, I suggest you do this performance on your knees."

There is no lack of leading conductors who barely reach my bellybutton, but on the podium these men stand ten feet tall and it has been a privilege to work with them.

Now what are these mysterious qualities that conductors must have to capture and hold us performers under their spell? Pierre Monteux had an unusual way of keeping your attention; he would deliberately underrehearse when working with seasoned professionals. I was to do Mephistopheles in *Faust* with him at the Met, and had not yet been introduced to the Maestro when I encountered him in the hall. I told him who I was and asked when I was going to rehearse the role with him, as the time was drawing short. He looked up at me with his cherubic smile and said, "You know the part, don't you?"

I said, "Well, yes, but I need to know how you do it."

He responded with, "If you wish...all right."

When I met with him a couple days later, he soon skipped about five pages of my music, but when I commented on this, he said pleasantly, "You know it, don't you?"

When I admitted I did, he proceeded without returning to the part we had omitted. This perplexed me until someone who had worked with him in the past informed me he deliberately underrehearsed with soloists as a matter of principle so as to keep their attention focused on him in performance.

Are there other forms of charisma that conductors can employ? Well, take the case of Dimitri Mitropoulos. He was to do the first *Boris* of his life at the Met, with me in the title role. My wife and I happened to run into him one night at the La Scala Restaurant in New York City and I approached him and introduced myself, mentioning how I was looking forward to preparing the *Boris* with him. He smiled his very charismatic best and said, "I am just there to be your accompanist!"

When Lucia and I walked out of the restaurant, she said archly, "Just there to be your accompanist? I'll bet. Just you wait!" And I had to laugh and go along with her experienced skepticism.

What a surprise, several months later, when I went to my first rehearsal with the Maestro. He and I were alone with the accompanist and he said, "Now, I will not conduct this rehearsal, I will simply take notes as to what you do." Surprise, surprise—he did just that!

What then, was his special quality? Well, for one thing, he conducted everything by memory and it was most impressive. In rehearsal without a score, he would instruct the orchestra to return to number 95, at the Andante Mosso. Everyone was astounded at his prodigious abilities. Add to this very impressive conducting skills and a charismatic personality, and you were completely won over.

These things lead us to realize that the great conductors seem to be very individualistic in their approach, and should we not expect that? So they are all different—and I say, *Vive la difference!*

But is there such a thing as an ideal conductor/singer relationship? It is very well-known that unpleasant situations can arise in which there is real conflict between the two and it can degenerate into a power struggle. I suppose that for there to be an ideal conductor/singer relationship you would have to have two impossible things: the ideal conductor and the ideal singer. It is unlikely we will ever find two such, but let us try to deal with the subject anyway.

Working with Emil Cooper was a very trying, yet rewarding experience. He was a storehouse of artistic knowledge, but he was also very impatient, especially with those young artists whom he felt were either not serious-minded, or properly prepared. He would often single out some inexperienced young American singer for crucifixion during a production and his attacks would be unrelenting. But, for some reason, I was destined to be one of his pets.

For example, during a rehearsal of *Peter Grimes*, I came in late on an entrance, throwing off a hapless colleague who was the next to enter. The Maestro began to fiercely harangue and castigate him for his lack of musicality. I interrupted to place the blame where it belonged—on myself. What was the Maestro's reaction? He smiled and gently said, "Think nothing of it. You're only human."

Now, as irrational and capricious as this makes Cooper sound, don't sell that little giant short: he simply could not waste his time on young artists who were superficial in their approach to music. In the middle of a rehearsal he would launch into a long seminar on the styles of composers or the challenge of understanding what was happening in the orchestra while one was singing. These lectures were obviously a big bore to many singers who would whisper, "Why doesn't he just tell us to sing loud or soft instead of going into these long speeches?"

Well, I used to enjoy and profit from these impromptu lectures; perhaps that is why I became a favorite of his. And Emil Cooper was the one who eventually taught me the ideal relationship between conductor and singer.

In the first three years that I performed with the Maestro at the Met, he never once allowed me to take the slightest liberty or think for myself. Then, when he was about to fulfill his biggest dream at the Met by not only conducting Moussorgsky's *Khovanshchina*, but also re-orchestrating at least two acts of it, he demanded that I be assigned the crucial role of Dossife.

After learning the role, I met with him to rehearse for the first time. When we had worked our way through to the main aria, I asked what was his tempo for it. He said, "No, what is your tempo?"

I stood there perplexed. I had no tempo. As always, I was expecting him to tell me what to do. He then continued, "You are the artist that must sing this role. You are supposed to have studied it in greater depth than even the conductor. In the aria you are King and must set your own moods and tempi and the conductor should follow you. In ensembles, the conductor is King and then you should follow him.

"Now, there is one spot in the aria where you enter after a fermata. For that one moment only, I must take the lead to keep both you and the orchestra together and then you take over again."

I was astonished at this turn of events and my new-found freedom. I came to realize that up to then the Maestro had regarded me as a gifted student, but a student nonetheless. Apparently, in his eyes, I had now graduated and become an artist—one who must now be encouraged to seek his own artistic freedom.

If conductors were to work exclusively with mature singers who could be trusted to do all things in good taste there would be many more opportunities for this ideal arrangement to spring up between conductor and singer. Unfortunately, it does not happen very often.

Regarding the extensive lectures some conductors are prone to deliver during rehearsals—pay heed—they can be most profitable. I recall verbatim a dissertation by Alberto Erede on Italian diction. On that occasion, I learned that in Italian the letter "r", when lying between two vowels, is always rolled with a single touch of the tongue. All other "r's" are pronounced as doubles.

I recall a lecture by Emil Cooper that surfaced during a rehearsal of *Aida* with Danize Illitch. Now, Madame Illitch was a most emotional performer and at one point she gave vent to a heartrending sob. Cooper stopped her:

"No, I do not think sobs are appropriate to Verdi. Different liberties go with different composers. That is known as the style of the composer. If you take liberties with rubatos and rallentandos in Mozart, it sounds like Rossini.

"You must be very careful about which liberties you take with each composer. With Verdi, it is a physical feat to sing high notes, so it is permissible to hold them longer than notated—but no sobs. Sobs belong in Puccini."

173

Do not complain when the conductor launches into a lecture. He probably has much to share with you, provided you have the intelligence to appreciate it.

A few words about the coaches. Bear in mind that the American singer is fundamentally being raised under a German school. That is fine for Mozart, Strauss, Wagner and any German repertoire, but it creates a serious problem with regard to Italian repertoire and the meaning of the word "legato." You will find no accord between Germans and Italians on the subject (and I know from fifty-eight years of experience in dealing with them). Any coach who will tell you that "legato" means getting as fast as you can from one note to the next, with no vulgar Italian slurs, is definitely of a German school.

Met coach, Jan Behr, and I argued many, many times about the meaning of this crucial word—and never could agree. I knew that he worshiped Fausto Cleva as a conductor and one day the three of us happened to meet in the hall. I quickly took advantage of the situation and asked Cleva to define the word "legato."

"Why," he said, "legato means 'tied together.' So, it is a small portamento between the notes." The shock on Jan's face was unmistakable.

To further complicate the matter, let me describe what happened one day when my wife, Lucia, delivered me the supreme putdown in front of Franco Corelli by saying, "Let's face it, Franco, these Americans are just not born to sing legato!"

That did it! I decided right then and there to come up with a logical approach to the subject and here is my conclusion: granted that legato has to do with sustaining the vowels as long as possible on each note (without stinting on the consonants—especially the double ones), it also deals with how to go from one note to the other. The trickiest part of the problem is going down from one note to the next when there is a consonant between the vowels. Suppose the word is "tanto" and it is sung on two different notes. The secret of Italian legato is that the "nt" is not pronounced until you are already on the pitch of the second note. It is that simple.

The same holds true when going higher in pitch if there is a legato mark above the phrase.

Coaches of the German-American school also have a misconceived notion of how Italian vowels should be pronounced. In the German language, one does not sing the Italian, open-throated "awe" vowel, nor is it used in French. In fact, all of the Italian vowels are produced with the lowered larynx, resulting in vowel sounds that are not the same as those in German and French.

The trouble is that our coaches are not usually aware of these important differences and think all vowels should be pronounced the same from language to language. When I joined the San Francisco Opera in 1941, I was called into the office of Herman Weigert, who was the chief coach for the *Tannhäuser* production. He was also the chief coach for the German wing of the Metropolitan Opera. He said, "Herr Hines, I am sorry to inform you that your vocal technique is completely wrong and you must find a new teacher." He then told me that my vowels were completely incorrect and he demonstrated the difference between the way I pronounced Italianized and rounded "ee", "eh" and "awe" vowels instead of the corresponding German ones. To him, singing the rounded vowels with the lowered larynx was a sign of bad technique. Fortunately, I shut my ears to his advice and continued my studies with Gennaro Curci with good result.

There is also the problem of singing in French on the opera stage. If you sing the vowels exactly as they are spoken, you will not be heard across the footlights. I remember when Edward Johnson produced *Pelléas and Mélisande* in the late forties and imported the world's two greatest leads from the Paris Opera for the title roles. They sang French most intimately, as it is pronounced in speaking. Well and good for small, intimate theatres, but in our 3,400 seat auditorium they were inaudible. After two performances, the rest were cancelled.

The problem is that the French language must be slightly

175

Italianized to be viable in the major opera houses. If you wish to disagree with me, then go argue with Jennine Reis, who is known as the foremost French coach in the world.

Jimmy Levine imported Jennine from Paris to coach us and himself when he did the first *Pélleas and Mélisande* of his life at the Met in the early eighties. I was pleased to find she concurred with the need of modification in the French language for big houses.

Italianization of the German vowels in Wagner is not essential. This one you can treat as you wish. I, personally, ran against the grain of the German coaches at the Met by my Italianization, but both Rudolf Bing and Wieland Wagner personally said that they preferred me in Wagner roles because I sang them with an Italian sound, which to their ears was more beautiful.

May you be so fortunate as to find coaches with a broad enough experience to know the critical difference between the proper vowel sounds inherent in each language and how they may occasionally be modified.

CHAPTER XIX

THE SINGING ACTOR

Ideally, an opera singer should be equally great as a vocalist and as an actor/actress, but a perfect balance between these two important roles is seldom achieved. And if one is to choose between the two, a great voice would probably be considered more important. Certainly one could not become a famous opera singer without having a minimal amount of voice, yet many artists have forged major careers without having a vestige of histrionic ability.

Opera singers, with rare exception, begin by studying voice. Some eventually turn to drama lessons, but drama always seems to take second place in the scheme of things. Ideally, voice and drama should share equal importance. However, this means that university and conservatory opera departments should offer drama classes intelligently geared to the special needs of opera, which differ from the needs of straight drama.

I had the rewarding experience of working with Margaret Webster in Rudolf Bing's production of *Don Carlo* singing both the roles of the Grand Inquisitor and Philip II. She was a brilliant director and her staging had a well-deserved success. I have seldom seen my colleagues act so well on stage and I have never seen the final struggle between Carlo and the royal guards look so believable—with Jussi Bjoerling as a most convincing swordsman!

Despite all the brilliance Margaret brought to the production, there were some musical expressions that called for dramatic action but were neglected. Ideally, an operatic stage director should carefully analyze the orchestral score and decide which musical phrases and chords belong to whom.

However, welding music and drama does create a problem: how detailed should the physical expression of the music be? Overdoing it is commonly called "Mickey Mousing." There was a period in the early sixties in which this problem was supposedly dealt with by having the dramatic expression occur just a moment after the musical one. That, of course, was nothing more than "delayed Mickey Mousing," which was no improvement at all. The resolution of this problem of "how much detail" must be left to good taste and judgment on the part of both the stage director and the artist.

I have had the pleasure of working with two true geniuses of operatic drama, Val Rosing and Frank Corsaro. These talented men taught young singers to act in distinctly different ways.

Val taught a system of exercises in classical body movement, based upon a principle similar to that found in Gestalt Psychology in which the organism must act as a whole, meaning that the spoken word was to be coordinated exactly with the gesture, not before or after. This also meant that the whole body had to say the same thing at the same time.

Val was able to sculpt the singer's body movements almost like a choreographer. He would have you try a certain action and if it did not fit you, he would say, "Darling, I'm a genius. I can do everything a thousand ways." And then he would block, sculpt and stage you until you were comfortable and effective. But working with Val was not as mechanical as I have made it sound: with him the mechanics were supplemental.

When I prepared the role of Philip II in Verdi's *Don Carlo* with Val, he had me start with my second act entrance, where a jealous and suspicious Philip finds his wife unattended in the garden, despite his orders to the contrary. As I stalked in from stage left, Val stopped me and asked where I had just come from.

"From the wings," I replied.

"That is just the way it looked," he responded. "Do it again."

When I entered again, he asked me the same question and I said, "I have just come from a meeting with the Grandees, who have followed me onstage."

"Why did you come to the garden?" he asked.

"To speak with the Queen," I shot back.

"What were you going to say to her?"

"I have no idea." My second shot was not too smart.

"Try it once more," he said, smiling broadly.

As I entered again, I was properly prepared to begin the scene, thinking that, as a result of our marriage of political convenience, Elisabetta had always been very cold to me. I had decided, as hard as it might be, to try just one more time to be nice and compliment her on how lovely she looked.

Then, when I discovered she was alone, against my orders, my resulting emotional explosion followed precipitately and harshly.

Val also had the singer decide in his/her imagination the importance of every piece of furniture, prop and window used on the stage. When I worked with Val on the monologue of *Boris Godunov*, and sang "How often have I heard it prophesied my power and my glory would be endless," Val asked me where the astrologer who predicted my future had been kneeling. We decided he had knelt in front of my throne and that I should now recall his presence there in my imagination.

Then, as I sang about the vanity of fame and the acclaim of the crowds, Val asked me to decide on the location of the window overlooking the Red Square from which I was accustomed to appear before the people. So, when I spoke of the allure of fame and the acclaim of the crowd, I was to relate to that window, and then in rejection of the thought, I was to turn away from it.

Next, when I saw the cameo of my daughter's dead fiancé on the table and thought about her terrible grief, Val suggested it would be natural to look at the door through which I had seen her leave. I then had to decide through which door she had just exited.

With this identification of things on the stage in your mind, the audience may not know exactly what you are thinking at the moment, but they will know that you look like a live human being in a real life situation.

Frank Corsaro employs a somewhat different approach. He never choreographs. He prepares you by asking you to imagine some real life experience of the past which is similar to the emotional experience you are portraying. You must be motivated to perform solely from your own deep subconscious.

Frank is also extremely brilliant at creating new and original interpretations of the text. Yet, no matter how unusual his staging, it is always soundly logical. I will give some examples of this in the following section on "The Stage Director." But now, more about individual artist's approaches to acting.

I had the distinct pleasure of working with the two greatest basso buffos of the past generation, and believe me, no two artists could be more antithetical. Salvatore Baccaloni was the "great comedian," Fernando Corena was the "great clown," and both were geniuses at what they did.

Baccaloni was sometimes criticized for his exaggerated pantomime but in his defense, how could a man be a successful comedian in a foreign language (we had no subtitles in those days) without a bit of exaggeration? The man was superbly funny and without equal in his day.

Impressed by his excellent acting ability, I once asked him if he ever improvised on stage. He responded: "Only fools improvise! I plan out every scene in at least five different ways and then, during the performance I choose at the last moment which one I will use."

Now, Baccaloni was never out of character, while Corena was seldom in it. Corena was either playing asides to the audience or striving to break up his colleagues on the stage. I know, because I tangled with Corena many a time on the stage. In retrospect, I must say it was never boring and certainly a challenge.

During a performance of *La Forza del Destino* on the Met tour, Fernando and I finished the Guardiano-Melitone duet and waited for the applause to die down, after which a bell was to ring off stage and I was to sing (in Italian), "Someone is here, open the gate."

The bell rang prematurely during the applause and Fernando, turning to me, cried out, "Telephone!" and ran off stage, leaving me to pick up the pieces.

On another occasion we were both cast in *Il Barbiere di Siviglia.* Before the show, Fernando saw me walking out of my dressing room eating a raw carrot. He was curious why, so I informed him raw vegetables were good for one's health and that he should try it.

Later, as I was on the stage singing the recitativo before "La Calunnia" in thundering tones, Fernando loudly observed in Italian, "Ah, you've been eating your salad?"

Then, as I began singing the aria, "La Calunnia," he started shushing me up, finally complaining loudly, "Take it easy, this theatre has good acoustics."

With that I decided to get my revenge and I did, but I will not waste your time with the details.

Whether you approved of Fernando Corena's bad boy tactics or not, he always had a big success. The audience loved him...and so did I.

But this kind of behavior is not always acceptable. In my early years at the Met, I was on the stage with Ramon Vinay, who was a truly superb actor. At one point in the performance, I turned my back to the audience and made a silly face, trying to break him up.

He looked at me and said quietly, "You are very funny."

He obviously did not think my antics were appropriate—and they were not! So, I learned an unforgettable lesson.

The Stage Director

This has become the generation of the stage director, the set designer and the conductor. It was not always so. A famous conductor said to me forty years ago, nobody comes to the opera house to see me conduct. They come to hear the great singers. It was the same then, regarding stage directors and set designers.

But now, all that has changed: you go to the Met to see Zeffirelli's *Traviata*, not Verdi's. Now, I don't mean to denigrate Zeffirelli's productions; they are spectacular. But, building the new Met at Lincoln Center caused a revolution in the way American opera is presented.

At the Old Met on 39th street, you hardly ever stood more than ten feet away from the prompter, because the stage was not very deep. In those days, a production of *Aida* required two truck loads of scenery, while *Il Barbiere di Siviglia* at the New Met several years later required twenty truck loads of scenery.

One cannot escape the fact that opera is presented on a bigger scale today than it was thirty years ago. And this means a greater importance is being given to stage directors and set designers. I must confess, I am not really happy with the change as a whole and I will explain why.

I was making a recording in London and my wife and I visited the British Museum where we saw some beautiful prints of still-life paintings on sale for about £1 apiece. We bought three of them and returned home to New Jersey, where my wife had them handsomely framed. I was delighted until I discovered that the frames cost fifty-five dollars apiece! Isn't it a bit odd to buy fifty-five-dollar frames for three-dollar prints? If the singers are to be regarded as the picture and the production as the frame, is that not exactly what we get in our major operatic productions these days?

Now, we tend to scoff at stage directors of the past who produced "instant opera," staging an entire production in one or two days. Yet many productions in which I participate today and which take three to four weeks to stage are no more interesting or innovative than the old ones. Sometimes those weeks are spent just teaching the stage director the opera.

It is a rarity to meet up with stage directors such as Val Rosing and Frank Corsaro, who are true geniuses and have done their homework. But it is also rare to encounter a brilliant vocalist who also shows some genius in acting. What is one to do when a singer of great vocal endowment leaves a bit to be desired in thespian abilities?

May I suggest that it might be worth while to sit there without complaining and revel in the sheer beauty of the sound that caresses your ears. Face the truth, fundamentally, opera is "voice, voice and more voice." And you can feel especially privileged whenever an artist with a great voice also happens to have great acting ability.

As to the singer/stage director relationship, I believe that every experienced artist should be listened to during the staging of an opera. Although the stage director must always have the final say, he/she should be wise enough to keep an open mind and hear the singer out.

Naturally, the stage director should bristle if an artist emphatically says, "This is the way I do it." At this point, I stand behind the stage director one hundred percent.

When Ezio Pinza was asked why he left the Met for South Pacific, his reply was, "What a bore to do the same old operas over and over again."

Frankly, I do not believe there are boring situations, only boring people. You should always strive to find new ways to do an opera you have done many times before. It is always a pleasure to meet up with a brilliant stage director who can supply a breath of fresh air to a hackneyed work.

The part I have sung the most is the title role in *Boris Godunov*. I first performed this role at the Old Met with only one staging

183

rehearsal in a private room and only one music rehearsal. I had just returned from an eight week tour of concerts which had taken me to my hometown of Los Angeles. While there, I hastily prepared *Boris* with Val Rosing, whom I consider to have been one of the most brilliant stage directors ever.

Earlier that season, Nicolai Rossi-Lemeni, George London and Cesare Siepi had already done the role of Boris and I was to be the fourth to undertake it. Obviously, I had to do something drastically different from them even to be noticed.

The key lay in the famous Clock Scene, where Feodor Chaliapin's classic staging included throwing a large chair at the clock where the ghost appeared and then knocking over a table and hiding beneath the tablecloth. Under Rudolf Bing, we were not allowed to smash clocks, so the staging at that time only retained crashing into the table, followed by the tablecloth bit.

Val Rosing's staging had Boris on his knees pleading with the ghost (indicated by a spotlight), which then circled him and sat upon the throne-chair as the true Tsar. Val then wanted me to pick up another chair and smash it down on the vision.

The idea was valid, but when I returned to the Met, Bing vetoed it, as he also did not want throne-chairs smashed. Compromising, I decided to pick up a knife from the table, threaten the ghost, then fearfully fall on my knees and plead for mercy. When that failed, I was to cry out, "Then die!" and run to the vision and plant the knife in the throne-chair, at which time the spotlight would go off. I would then scream in horror and collide with the table and do the classic finale. The power of this innovation lay in having Boris reenact the murder of the Tsarevich in his own imagination.

This staging was so successful that I began to repeat it everywhere I went—and, of course, began to fall into the trap of saying, "This is the way I do it."

Fortunately, I met up with a brilliant stage director, David Rizzo, who was determined I was not going to get away with doing it "My Way." So, every suggestion I made, he automatically shot down, determined to have it "His Way." Just as stubbornly, I began to resist all of his planned staging. Soon, everything came to grinding halt. Then we both reluctantly agreed to come up with something completely original and mutually acceptable. We began to create together and the result was far different from anything I had ever seen done in *Boris* before—and was highly successful.

Earlier in the act, I had ordered my son Fyodor out of the room. After the famous Mad Scene began with the ticking of the clock and with the spectre about to appear, the big double doors at the rear of the stage slowly opened to reveal the ghostly figure of a child. Terrified by this "vision," I was to run across the stage, knocking over the table and hiding myself under the cloth. I screamed in terror as the child ran across to me and clutched my arm. Only then did I realize that what I had supposed was the ghost was actually my own son, Fyodor, returning to bid me goodnight.

What a brilliant twist to the classic finale of this scene and what a beautiful example of creative cooperation between soloist and stage director. The number of ways a theme can be varied is endless, depending upon the genius of the stage director and the flexibility of the performing artist.

Now consider the genius of Frank Corsaro. I had been won over by his brilliant staging of *L'Amore dei Tre Re* in Washington, D.C. and insisted on having him stage the New Jersey State Opera's *Boris*.

Again, a brilliant, innovative finale emerged for the Clock Scene. Frank assumed that Boris had never actually seen the ghost, but only dreamt about it. He wanted Boris to fervently seek a face-to-face encounter with the ghost in order to plead his innocence.

Frank staged the scene in the children's playroom, instead of in the traditional throne room. There was a large armchair on a platform in the middle of the stage, with its back to the audience and a broad stairway going up on stage left. When Boris heard Prince Shuisky describe the bloodied corpse of the murdered Tsarevich clutching a little doll as though protecting it, he threw Shuisky out and collapsed halfway up the stairs.

Bright footlights came on, throwing huge shadows on the walls and from the large chair one saw a child's arm appear with a toy doll clutched in its hand. Boris reacted with a choked "Ah, there you are, in the chair."

The child got up, its back to the audience and circled around to stage right and began to approach Boris, holding out the toy as if to give it to him. Boris ran to the child and fell on his knees before him, grasping his shoulders, trying to plead his innocence. The child smiled sweetly at Boris and slowly raised his head. Then Boris saw the child's throat was horribly slashed from ear to ear and sprang to his feet with a scream of horror as the child disappeared.

Boris, staring at his hands, covered with the child's blood, then cried out to God to be merciful to the guilty Tsar.

While I believe a singer's attitude should be to seek fresh ways of doing older works, I simply cannot abide the idea of a stage director being outrageously different just for the sake of attracting attention. Innovative staging should serve the opera, not the director's ego.

I believe staging should basically be logical as well as theatrical. I have nothing against abstraction, provided some sort of message is distinguishable and sensible. For me, a clash of styles simply does not make sense. What connection is there between the nineteenth-century music of *Rigoletto* and a twentieth-century story line and twentieth-century style of dress? Such artistic miscegenation reveals a paucity of creative ability in this generation. If we want to produce a modern work, we should not distort a classic, but create a new one! I love to surprise an audience, but not to shock it to the point of losing the continuity of the drama. A good example of this would be a production I did of *Man of La Mancha* where the Abduction Scene (also called the Rape Scene) was so strongly over done that when we began the next scene (called the Gypsy Scene) we found all the people in the audience staring at each other incredulously, and asking, "Did you see what I just saw?" They were totally oblivious of what was happening on the stage.

They were so out of it that it took us several minutes to get their attention back to the stage again. The extreme audacity of the stage director and choreographer served themselves, not the production.

The producer subsequently got so many phone calls in protest that he temporarily cut the Rape Scene out of the show. He also got a fair amount of protest from me. It then became quite obvious from public response that the show was much more successful when the audience's sensibilities were not so deeply offended.

This, of course, will bring a knee-jerk reflex of hysterical protest from those great defenders of "freedom of expression." We immediately hear that "censorship" is a "four-letter word" and must be stamped out. Let us examine this in the cold light of reason.

In the early fifties, the use of profanity was totally unacceptable in the media. When performing on the radio, we could not sing "And to hell with Burgundy," but had to substitute "Down, down, down with Burgundy." Clark Gable saying, "Frankly, my dear, I don't give a damn" was the big shocker and signaled the beginning of the end for American censorship—at least, that is what we are led to believe.

The big battle began between the movie business and the newly innovated television industry. The motion-picture companies fought television violently, fearing it would destroy their business. One tool they began employing was presenting movies so offensive to current moral standards that they could not be brought into the home on the TV screen. Their films were often designed to drag the public out to their ailing movie houses through controversy.

By the early seventies, anything could be done on the stage, no matter how sexually explicit, or violent, or filled with foul and offensive language. This was supposed to convince us that censorship no longer had a place in our modern and enlightened society.

Now, take a look at the facts. When I did *South Pacific* in the eighties, I was told I could not use the original script in which I refer to "the Japs," but had to call them "the Japanese." Of course, this makes little sense in the context of the original show, which is set in a time of war, and when we were not given to being polite when

187

referring to the enemy. Other lines also had to be deleted. When referring to my late Polynesian wife, I was not allowed to say, "I came here as a young man, I lived as I could." That was a racial slur.

But these problems extended to more than just plays and musicals, but to classics as well. When singing in Mozart's *The Magic Flute*, I could not say to Monastatos, "Go, your soul is as black as your face." I was also informed that "Women's Lib" would be offended if Sarastro told Pamina, "By man your course must be decided, for by herself a woman steps beyond her sphere and is misguided." In fact, the entire story of *The Magic Flute* would be an offence to Women's Lib.

Now where does that leave us? Are not the above examples clearly censorship? Sure they are: we used to speak of the "D...word" and the "F...word," but now it is the "N.....word."

Censorship will always be with us, it is only the moral code that changes. Being regularly used, even in comic strips, profanity is now "in" while ethnic slurs are definitely "out." And is not suppression of antisocial activities such as murder and thievery a form of censorship?

So, when the so-called liberals cry out for "freedom of expression," they are liars and hypocrites. Without some form of rational censorship there is no civilization.

Chapter XX

The Manager

One of the greatest problems facing the young singer is how to secure a manager. Going from the conservatory to the professional stage always conjures up the Catch-22 scenario in which singers cannot secure good engagements without managers and managers pay no attention to singers who are not already accomplishing something important.

I was a twenty-five-year-old performing Mephistopheles in *Faust* with the Metropolitan Opera when Sol Hurok offered me a contract. How did I get as far as the Met without a manager? Things were different in those days; we did not go to conservatories; our maestros taught privately, and often acted as our managers until we made it in the profession.

In today's world, how do you get a Metropolitan Opera contract without a manager? And before you seek a manager are you sure you are ready for a career? Being the graduate of a major conservatory is no guarantee that you are. Let me ask a few pertinent questions.

Are you properly prepared to sing major roles in the average American opera company?

Do you know at least fifteen complete major roles of the "bread and butter" repertoire and could you perform any one of those roles on twenty-four hours notice?

Does your command of the languages in your repertoire include *excellent* diction and an understanding of the text, not just by the sentence, but word by word?

Have you found the right repertoire for your voice? (It is futile for singers with lyric voices to delude themselves into believing they have "spinto" or dramatic voices. I don't care how good it feels to sing heavy repertoire in the studio if your voice disappears when singing in a large hall with a full orchestra in the pit.)

Now to the manager. Just as singers must have fully developed skills, so must managers. But what should you look for in a manager? While managers can audition you, unfortunately you cannot audition them. So appraising a manager's skills is quite difficult.

In my opinion all managers should have the creative ability to tailor unique and innovative presentations for each specific artist. It was Sol Hurok who first suggested I do dramatized concerts, the first half with a classical recital format and the second half in costume and makeup, equipped with mirror, props and makeup tray on the piano. He wanted me to change from one character to another in front of the audience, along with running dialogues to explain each character I was about to portray. When the recital business began to die due to the advent of television, this innovative format helped me survive in the business longer than most.

When Sol Hurok died, I went under the management of my longtime friend, James Sardos, who has a wonderfully creative mind. His innovative ideas have had much to do with the longevity of my career, for which I am most grateful. He and I have made a good team for the past twenty-five years.

A manager must also have a deep concern for the artist as a person. Sol Hurok took me out to lunch at least once a year, always inquiring about my family and asking if I were saving a significant part of what I was earning.

James Sardos had been a close friend of mine since my debut at the Met. He was one of the most fervent opera lovers I have ever known. When I was contracted for a new role under his management, he would call me on the phone to see if I had learned it yet and would even test me by singing my cues.

These were great managers and may you be blessed by finding someone equally good.

When you feel you are ready for the profession, then be warned: if you are sick or in poor voice on the day of an audition, cancel. Once they have heard and rejected you, it is very unlikely they will ever be willing to hear you again.

One problem you will immediately face is that the big music centers such as New York City are teeming with good singers who all deserve a career but most of whom will never end up on the stage. While there are thousands of talented singers in New York's Tri-State area alone, the tragic fact is that the total number of Americans who earned $25,000 or more singing opera in the entire U.S.A. in 1994 was only 104.

Another problem is that a singer should ideally have three voice lessons and two or three coachings every week, which could cost between $2,000 and $2,500 a month—and where is such money to be found? Add to that the brutal fact that many managers (but not all) charge young, unknown singers a retainer which can run anywhere from $2,000 to $12,000 per year (not including expenses for telephone calls, flyers and advertising in music magazines).

Despite all these drawbacks, assuming that you have signed with a manager, do not expect him or her to do your job in addition to theirs. The manager's responsibility is to get you auditions, *not jobs*! It is your responsibility to be so spectacular that the impresario will be compelled to hire you. So, if your manager gets you the auditions and you do not get the jobs, blame yourself, not your manager.

There are various kinds of contracts you can sign with a manager. If you sign an exclusive worldwide contract, realize that if you secure an engagement independent of your manager, you are legally bound to pay your manager 20 percent of your concert fees and 10 percent of your opera fees.

If a European manager secures an overseas engagement for you and refuses to split the percentage with your American manager, or vice-versa, you will end up paying a double fee, or losing the engagement.

If you have reason to believe your manager has no clout in Europe, then it does not pay to sign an exclusive worldwide contract when one for the continental U.S.A. would do.

Another problem lies in deciding whether to go with a prominent manager with a big list, or a lesser known one. If the important managers have too many artists on their lists, you might get lost in the crowd. But the small manager may not have enough connections and clout to get you important auditions. I know of no way to definitively address this problem. If you find the answer, please let me know.

CHAPTER XXI

THE IMPRESARIO

Ezio Pinza used to tell an interesting story about a young tenor who had made a brilliant debut in a major theater. The impresario summoned the tenor to his office and told him how pleased he was and offered him a lucrative contract for the next season. He said the contract would be ready to sign in a week.

Two days later, the tenor was suddenly called upon to substitute that very evening for another singer who had been taken ill and rushed to the hospital. The young man told the impresario that he could not possibly sing because he himself had suddenly come down with a severe windpipe infection and could barely talk.

The impresario pleaded with him to reconsider because there was no one else available and, if he did not sing, there would be no performance.

The tenor desperately tried to squirm out of it, knowing he

would do not well, but the impresario kept pressing him, saying that they would understand his condition and would be eternally grateful if he could save the situation; it was a dire emergency and he simply had to help them out.

So, the tenor reluctantly agreed to sing, but asked the impresario to announce to the public that he was indisposed. The impresario insisted it was better not to call attention to his condition, saying no one would really notice.

The poor fellow struggled his way through the performance and the next day, the critics slaughtered him in the press.

When the time came for the tenor to sign his new contract, the impresario said to him, "How can you expect us to take you back next season after the terrible reviews you got?"

"But, you said you would understand," the tenor protested. "I did it to help you out! You insisted that I sing!"

"My boy," said the impresario, "when I insisted, I was only doing my job. You should have done yours and said 'No!'"

Obviously, the moral of the tale is know when to say "No!" And you, the singer, will have many such difficult decisions to make.

There can be other difficult decisions in which you have to know when to say "Yes." A most unusual case involved a soprano with whom I had worked extensively in the past. She had sung all over Europe, specializing in the title role of a very rare opera. She had tried many times to get on the Met roster, but was never able to break through, and now they were producing the rare work which she had sung so often. One day, the diva singing the title role at the Met had to cancel on the day of the show and there was no one else on the roster that knew it well enough to go on. They quickly called my friend and offered her that night's performance.

Unfortunately, she had a bad cold and knew she would not do well. Should she say "Yes" or "No"? She felt it was unlikely that the Met would ever hire her in the future, so she decided to sing. Why? Because she would acquire something no one could ever take away from her: the Met name!

What would you have done?

There is yet another problem inherent in both these situations that we should discuss. When a singer is indisposed, should an announcement be made to the public? For some unexplained reason, impresarios strongly advise against this practice. Perhaps they feel it will reflect badly on them for not having an adequate cover waiting in the wings. Whatever the reason, they are usually against it.

In my own experience, every time I was indisposed and sang without an announcement, I paid dearly for it.

As a bitter example, I was doing a matinee performance of *Boris* with a major symphony on the East Coast and came down at the last moment with strong, unpleasant symptoms. The symphony management had me examined backstage, before the show, by a doctor who was on their board of directors. He decided I had the mumps, of all things, then went on to say, "I should quarantine you, but it would be a disaster for the symphony to cancel the concert at the very last moment."

He then instructed me to go ahead and sing, but not to tell anyone what I had. He also instructed me not to shake hands with anyone after the concert, but get in my car, drive straight home (a five hour trip), get in bed and call my family doctor.

Well, in such a situation, I could in no way announce my indisposition. So, I sang, and badly. My wife came back stage after the concert and quoted people in the lobby as saying, "I didn't know Jerome Hines sounded like that!"

I was never invited back to sing with their orchestra again. That was really a trap! So, I strongly advise my fellow soloists to always insist on letting the public and the critics know when they are not up to par.

But do not get in the habit of "crying wolf" every time you set foot on the stage, or you will get a bad reputation, and that can be quite harmful. Take a judicious approach to the matter—but do protect yourself.

Now, let me take the impresario's point of view for a moment. In recent years, I have seen the battlefield from the other side. Serving for eight years as general manager and artistic director of Opera Music Theatre International (OMTI), an internship program for extraordinarily gifted young singers, has convinced me that you singers are NUTS! Well, most of you! I now understand much better why some singers with colossal talent never have a career.

First of all, it pays to try and understand what an impresario is going through at any given moment. In many cases, a company or symphony may be going through hard times financially. It is most important that you cooperate with them on fundraising luncheons, interviews, etc. Also the reception after the performance is the one opportunity for volunteers and sponsors to get a little reward by meeting the artists. Consider this sort of activity to be an unwritten part of your contract.

Remember, the impresario faces great stress, just as the performing artist does. But it is a different sort of stress and can be truly devastating. In my eight short years managing OMTI, I faced situations in which I had never before felt so helpless.

Imagine, beginning to put up a tent for a $75,000 opera performance honoring Governor Tom Kean of New Jersey, who had made our OMTI program possible, and then being informed that a hurricane was coming and erecting the tent was impossible!

Or imagine having irrevocably invested over $200,000 in a Maurice Sendak production of *The Magic Flute* and being told by the theater management that the sets were 20,000 pounds too heavy for their grid and we would have to cancel the show!

The next time you find your impresario a bit edgy, give him a shoulder to cry on. I do not mean to say that the impresario is always right, but again, be judicious and try to get to the truth—and be cooperative and understanding when it is called for.

Chapter XXII

The Critic

Over the years, critics have meant many things to me: at times they have been of value; at times they have left me puzzled; at times they have been a real source of humor; at other times they have been a big pain in the you know what.

Anyhow, I have survived three generations of critics and have come up with a mixed bag of memories both happy and not so happy—with scars aplenty to show for it.

Now, as much as we performers tend to malign critics, I have to admit they are essential, and I thank God for the good ones. Regarding the others, we should probably refuse to dignify those who are nothing more than "professional scorners" with the title of "critic." However, in our rush to paste the label of "professional scorner" on a critic, we must bear in mind that there are also good singers and bad singers, and the bad ones often deserve to be scorned. So I am not going to devote this chapter to critic-bashing, but I will try to find a path to peaceful coexistence between critic and performer which will be fair to both.

In my dealings with critics, I have become aware of several basic problems that we should discuss in depth:

Objective vs. Subjective Criticism

In the mid-sixties, as my wife and I were walking down a hallway in the Teatro Colon of Buenos Aires, we saw the new general manager, Maestro Valenti-Ferro approaching us. In the early fifties, we had known him as Argentina's leading music critic. We greeted each other warmly and chatted a few moments. Before we parted, my wife asked Valenti-Ferro a question that took me by surprise, and surely him as well.

"Maestro," she said, "now that you have been the General Manager of Teatro Colon for a while, could you ever go back to being a critic again?"

He thought deeply for a moment, and then replied with a sad, whimsical smile, "No! I just...did not understand!"

This encounter draws attention to the Great Divide that yawns between the performer and the critic and raises all sorts of questions. Would it be of value for a critic to first serve as a professional artist, an impresario or a manager? Would it be of value for artists to submit in advance an outline of how they intended to interpret the music? And would critics review a performance differently had they been privy to all the facts and circumstances behind the scenes?

Many critics say they do not want to be influenced by anything except what was objectively seen and heard in the performance. Is that a rational stand to take? Consider the two following encounters I had with important critics:

I sang the role of Swallow in a revival of *Peter Grimes* during the Met's 1983/84 season and got excellent reviews from all the New York newspapers. Then, I was quite surprised to find the following:

⌐ The Critic ⌐

The New Yorker, Nov. 8, 1983—by Andrew Porter
Jerome Hines, who has been singing Swallow at the Met for
35 years, still mispronounces "quietus" (not a mere British
quibble—a glance at Webster would put him right)

That was the sum total of his review of my performance. So, I
sent Mr. Porter my "review" of his review:

Quietus Hiatus

Subject—The word "quietus" as sung by Jerome Hines in
the Metropolitan Opera production of *Peter Grimes* in the
1983-84 season.
Pronunciation of "Quietus"—1. Latin (Kwietoos)
　　　　　　　　　　　　　　　2. English (Kwietus)
　　　　　　　　　　　　　　　3. Hines (Kwiatus)
Memo—(Sept. 29, 1983)—Bodo Igesz, stage director of
Peter Grimes to Jerome Hines—"Swallow, a country lawyer,
probably learned the word "quietus" only yesterday. Using
the word portentously, he mispronounces it. I believe that
answers your question, Jerry."
Deed (or misdeed, according to one's understanding)
committed on Oct. 13, 1983—Jerome Hines, having adequate
foreknowledge of both the Latin and Webster pronunci-
ations of "quietus," deliberately chooses to sing
"*Kwiatus*" so it will be *neither-nor*.
Review (Nov. 9, 1983)—Jerome Hines re Andrew Porter—

"His sense of hearing is nonpareil;
his sense of humor nonexistent."

Comment—Dear Andrew, if you print this it will belie my
review, just as I have belied yours.

JEROME HINES

199

(Porter answered me in a personal letter with a friendly, humorous reply, but my "review" of his review was never printed—that is, until now.)

What conclusion can we draw from this example? Mr. Porter had no inside information telling him that I was deliberately mispronouncing the word, so he missed the point as to why it was mispronounced. Instead, he took me to task, assuming I acted through ignorance. This sort of error will always creep in when there is no advance communication between the artist and the critic. This is but one of the dangers inherent in purely objective criticism.

The Little-Knowledge Critic is Dangerous

Now for another review that was even more frustrating: a sarcastic and incompetent coverage of Metropolitan Opera performances of *Parsifal* and *Don Carlo* in one of America's leading music publications by a critic from London (who shall remain nameless) and who was out to prove the Metropolitan Opera could not hold a candle to Covent Garden. The only artist the critic liked in both *Parsifal* and *Don Carlo* was Herman Uhde, a regular at Covent Garden. I have no complaints about Uhde, who was a fine artist and colleague. But the way he was used against the rest of us was extremely biased and uncomplimentary. The critic's excesses in the matter finally reached the ridiculous.

The critic claimed that the grand climax of the Met's *Don Carlo* came when Uhde, as the Grande Inquisitor, recognized the voice of Carlo Quinto in the closing scene. Let me now spill the beans about the "grand climax" of that performance.

Being in the second cast of that production, Uhde had only one staging rehearsal, which did not include the two acolytes which were to lead him on and off stage in each scene. When Uhde came on stage in the final act, he wanted the acolytes to let go of his arms after he was in place. It had not originally been staged that way, so when he tried to shake them loose, they held on tenaciously. He became upset and tried all the harder to extricate himself, whispering harshly to them, "weg, weg." They obviously had no idea what "weg" meant and clung to him all the tighter. Just then Louis Sgarro sang the lines of the mysterious Frate and immediately following this came the "grand climax" in which Uhde was to recognize the voice of the Frate as that of Carlo Quinto. But he was so distracted by the acolytes that, instead of singing "E la voce di Carlo," out came "E la voce di Sgarro!" (It is the voice of Sgarro!) With that, everyone on the stage literally curled up in hysterics.

There are two problems with this reviewer. First of all, it was a blatant example of subjective criticism in which the critic was more interested in damning the Metropolitan Opera than in writing a fair review. The second problem was that the critic knew something about the opera *Don Carlo* but, apparently, dangerously little about the Italian language!

Judge, Jury and Executioner

I have a great appreciation for the critic who smacks me for something I know I did not do well. First of all, it proves that I am dealing with a knowledgeable colleague. But I cannot appreciate the reviewer who irresponsibly usurps the positions of judge, jury and executioner. When criticizing a performer, instead of simply reviewing the performance, some critics cannot resist waxing pontifical, and run the risk of stepping beyond the bounds of responsible criticism. Let me give you two contrasting examples of what I consider responsible and irresponsible criticism:

I sang Mephistopheles in *Faust* over a bad cold in Edmonton, Alberta. In spite of a windpipe infection, I sang quite decently except in the high voice, which was stiff and tight. The reviewer gave me a reasonably good notice and mentioned that my high voice was not what it should be, which indicated to me that I was dealing with a colleague whose opinion could be trusted.

In contrast to this, several years earlier, when I had just passed the devastating age of fifty, I did a concert in my hometown of Los

Angeles, again with a windpipe infection. As in the Canadian performance, I had to struggle to produce my high voice and was grateful just to get through the performance. The reviewer informed the public that Jerome Hines, now that he was over fifty, could no longer sustain his high voice. Needless to say, my high voice was back in excellent condition in a week or so when the edema from the infection had subsided (and still is at the age of seventy-five). This was a perfect example of the judge, jury and executioner syndrome. It is irresponsible journalism, and should be answered.

Believe it or not, I meant it before when I said "I have great appreciation for the critic who smacks me for something I know I did not do well." As a good example of this, in the earlier years of my career, I received such rave reviews from Philadelphia's world-renowned critic, Max De Schauensee that it seemed I could do no wrong. Max and I eventually got to such a friendly stage that he invited my wife and me to his apartment to hear some recordings he himself had made as a singer.

The next season, I sang a concert at the Academy of Music. Driving home, my wife said, "Darleeng, you did not seeng well tonight. But don't worry, Max is a friend and surely he weell go easy on you."

My reply surprised her:

"If Max goes easy on me for this concert, I will never believe him again when he gives me a good review."

Well, Max really hit me for that concert—and it delighted me. A year later he reviewed me most favorably in an operatic performance and I was comfortable in believing I had done well.

A Love/Hate Relationship

After a Civic Music concert in Newburgh, New York, I attended a cocktail party and entered into conversation with O.O. Bottorf, the president of Civic Concert Service, Inc.

"Jerome," he said, fixing me with a cold stare, "You get some of the worst reviews of any artist on our list."

I stood there speechless, wondering what was coming next. He continued:

"And, Jerome, you get some of the greatest reviews of any artist on our list. I don't know what it is you do to the critics: they either hate you or love you, but they simply cannot ignore you. Whatever you are doing, boy, don't change. I personally know of three critics who lost their jobs because of the great public outcry on how unjustly they had treated you. Keep it up, fella, don't change."

It is true, most of my reviews were highly favorable, but I also drew headlines like "Sold Down the River," or "Could Be God Really Sings Via Jerome Hines?" Oh, there have been some dillies.

As to the first headline, that was simply a critic's disagreement with me on how a recital should be programmed and there is nothing irresponsible about that (even though the headline was a bit sensationalized). But, you might just wonder where that second headline came from. That one requires some clarification. I will let you be the judge.

I was going to produce my opera *I Am the Way* with the Indianapolis Symphony in the fall of 1967. I had been independently booked there for a recital six months earlier and the gentleman who was heading the committee to promote the opera decided to host a dinner before the concert as a kick-off for the production. Included among the guests was Charles Staff, critic for the Indianapolis News. The gentleman heading the opera committee asked me how I prepared myself to sing the role of the Christ. I said that I had paid a visit to Joseph Meier who had created the famous Black Hills Passion Play and had performed the role of Jesus over two thousand times. He said the only way he could approach the role was to simply pray that the Lord would Himself play the role through him. And that was the approach I adopted.

Now, the way I prepare myself to sing the role of Jesus Christ has nothing to do with how I deliver a recital. Nonetheless, in reviewing the next day's concert, Mr. Staff began:

Could Be That God Really Sings Via Jerome Hines?
… information of this sort puts a reviewer in a rather delicate position. It is one thing to criticize Hines and quite another to direct 'helpful hints' to God.

Now, is that an objective, responsible review of a recital? You be the judge! (And you just imagine what kind of a review he gave to *I Am the Way* six months later!)

The Critic/Performer Relationship
One thing that has deeply disturbed me over the years is the imbalance in the critic/performer relationship which derives from an unfair practice of exclusively *criticizing singers yet not criticizing critics*. Such a situation is no more healthy or more rational than having a debate with only one participant. The unpleasant consequence of such an imbalance is the opportunity for some critics to declare an "open season" on performers—the bigger the game, the bigger the prize! Then, the bloodied performer is supposed to crawl away and silently bleed to death instead of retaliating.

For a short time, the Met was privileged to have Dimitri Mitropoulos in the pit, and when he did his first *Boris Godunov* there, I was privileged to sing the title role. It was a memorable experience for me. When Mitropoulos went on the Met tour for the first time, and his performance was reviewed at Indiana University, we all were shocked to see the student newspaper come out with the headline:

"MITROPOULOS DISAPPOINTING"

Obviously, the brash, inexperienced kid who wrote that review was only out to prove he was a David slaying his Goliath. His only concern was to feed the fires of his own ego and not to serve the cause of great music. If he is still writing today, he has probably developed into what I previously referred to as a "professional scorner." I hope, instead, he has chosen a more fitting profession—such as a Sanitation Engineer.

Don't think for a moment that I want the singer to be immune from attack. Public performance should be criticized in public. My advice to the performer is if you don't want to be criticized publicly, stay off the stage. But, I feel that a healthy balance between performer and critic could be found if one basic change were to be made in the way we function. We should take our cue from the way politics is handled by the media: the performer should be given "equal time" or, in this case, equal space.

In fifty-five years of career, only six times did I so strongly feel that a critic had stepped beyond the bounds of responsible criticism that I responded with a letter to the editor. In each case, the editor printed my rebuttal, with the sole exception of the *New York Times* (which was a disappointment since I expected more of the Times; and I also I felt I had written a pretty good piece which deserved to be printed).

I have tried out this idea of rebuttal on several eminent critics, including Joseph McClellan on the *Washington Post* and David Stabler on the *Oregonian* in Portland. To my pleasant surprise, they all responded positively to it. Stabler's comment was, "If we critics knew we were going to be answered by the artist, we would probably be a lot more careful about what we write."

The Purist

Occasionally we artists have to face purists so pure that it is hard to believe they were actually spawned on a planet plagued with original sin. Their quest for the perfection reflected in their own image takes many forms. For example, a performance can be completely ruined by the impurity of the English language which, incidentally, was good enough for Shakespeare and his ilk. Consider this review from Vancouver:

November 17, 1958
Vancouver Symphony—Orchestra Concert
The Province—Ian Docherty

When Mr. Hines joined the orchestra for his first group of arias—by Verdi, Mozart and Gounod, he revealed a voice as impressive in size and range as his own six feet, six inches of height.

DESPITE THE impressive physical aspect of his voice, the singer rarely struck any vital spark in these arias. In the Mozart he committed the parochial error of singing in English...

The final part of the program was devoted to excerpts from Modeste Moussorgsky's *Boris Godunov*...

"BORIS GODUNOV" sung in English...is reduced to mere black and white, from its inherent rich reds and purples. Moussorgsky wrote vocal music so closely aligned with the Russian language that to translate it into any other tongue is a complete waste of time...

It would be interesting to know if Mr. Docherty speaks any Russian at all. But, I am happy to report that I was able to get a slight degree of revenge as we repeated the concert the following evening. Also scheduled on the program was my vocal setting of the "Twenty-Third Psalm." I stopped the conductor just as he was playing the introduction and announced that I wished to offer a personal apology to Ian Docherty, the offended purist, for not performing the "Twenty-Third Psalm" in the multi-hued colors of the original Hebrew. Now contrast this with another review of the same concert:

November 17, 1958
King Edward H.S., Vancouver Symphony—Concert
Blue and White—Joan Arnold

Mr. Hines used his deep, resonant voice to full advantage in a moving performance of excerpts from "Boris Godunov." This performance proved that opera can be successfully sung in English without losing any of its original vitality.

206

Now, let us indulge in a little more musicological Puritanism:

January 22, 1959

Boston Morning Musicales—Recital

Boston Globe—Cyrus Durgin

In the ballroom of the Statler Hilton Hotel yesterday the Metropolitan Opera bass was in his best form, which means a glorious voice, vigorous performance and a personality which captures and steadily holds interest...

Speaking for myself, I wish Hines did not feel obliged to insert, as encore midway in a program, such a corny item as Moussorgsky's "Song of the Flea"...

October 31, 1960

Curran Theater, San Francisco—Recital

San Francisco Chronicle—Dean Wallace

Physically, Hines is large enough to go bear hunting with a bowie knife, and he has a voice scaled to the same grand proportions. For all its size and volume, one marvels at the agility, accuracy, and ease of production which make it capable of some extremely delicate sounds.

This magnificent instrument has been put to the uses of grand opera, and like many operatic voices, it suffers somewhat from its owner not being overty [overly] aware of what is best for it. Hines sang the usual polyglot potpourri type of program ranging from maroque [Baroque] arias to Negro spirituals—the kind of program singers should reserve for the provinces, if retained at all, especially since it offers a discriminating audience as much opportunity to wince at a singer's faults as to bask in his virtues. Moreover, it produces several abrupt changes of mood, which serves first to frustrate, then to bore.

The Public as Critic

Over the years, the most important critic in my life has been the audience. I have never been able to buy the argument that the general public is stupid. If there is no audience, there is no show. Art is created to serve people; people were not created to serve Art.

What is the public's role in the world of serious music? Can we trust them to be the final arbiter of what is good and bad in serious music? If so, then what is the place of the educated visionary and missionary of the classics, the musicologist? Is he, instead of the public, the one to be entrusted with the future of the Arts, particularly if he seems to be completely out of step with everyone else? Does that mean the public is stupid? Not in my opinion. How does one resolve this conflict between the musicologist and the general public for whom the music is really intended? I have a possible solution.

In 1947, I performed my first public recital at The Redlands Bowl in Southern California. The day after the concert, I was confronted by my teacher, Gennaro Curci, who felt I had programmed the recital badly and that we should start from scratch. I went to his studio and as fate would have it, my mother accompanied me there. Now, let me go on record as saying that with all my dear mother's good qualities, music appreciation was not one of them. She would not have walked across the street to see an opera nor hear a concert unless her son were appearing in it. Her forceful-ways and opinions often irked the Maestro, and he usually referred to her as "Madame The President."

Curci began the session by suggesting I consider the early Italian song "Amarilli" for the new program. After playing it he waited for my reaction. Mother bluntly said, "I don't like it."

Curci was visibly miffed. "One of the great Italian classics and 'Madame The President' doesn't like it," he growled sarcastically. He then turned to another early Italian classic.

When he finished playing it, mother responded with, "I like it." That seemed to rile the Maestro even more. It irked him that mother was setting herself up as self-appointed music critic. And there I was, caught in the cross-fire. At first I found the situation rather amusing, but then it dawned on me that there was pay dirt here. This was a classic case of a sophisticated musicologist versus the common public. But that raises the question, "For whom do we artists perform, a house full of music critics and musicologists, or the general public?" Curci considered my mother to be a musical illiterate and that is exactly what she was. Did that mean her opinion was of no value? What possible credence could be given to my mother's uneducated opinion?

Then the truth struck me: "It doesn't take a chicken to know a good egg." I suddenly realized that songs which would please *both* Curci and my mother would be the answer. And, in general, I have always tried to program my recitals in such a manner that they would please *both* the musicologist *and* the general public.

Yes, I appreciate the scrupulous, responsible critic but I am not ashamed of welcoming the general public's opinion as well.

In Conclusion

I would advise singers to pay careful attention to their reviews for the purpose of detecting common trends in what the critics have written. If you are accused more than once or twice of having certain vocal or musical problems, you could check up on yourself by having someone tape each of your performances. Then you too would become a critic, but in a very constructive sense.

If you are being reviewed in a production involving other soloists, check your own opinions about them and see if they agree with what the critic has to say. If you agree with the critic's opinions about the others, you had better pay attention to what the critic has to say about you.

See that your manager is given all reviews that have even one decent word to say about you, because a good manager will know how to skillfully extract something positive that can be included in an up-to-date flyer to send to the impresarios.

Try to catch the mood of the critic. On occasion a reviewer will be out to hate and destroy everything and everyone in sight: the sets are ridiculous, the costumes are amateur, the conductor and orchestra are sloppy, and the soloists are either miscast or simply don't know how to sing! Tear the review up and forget it, it's not worthy of being used in the bathroom.

Finally, do not expect everyone to love you. No matter how great you may be, someone will be waiting to kill you for some outlandish reason. Be patient and follow my example: I have survived at least three generations of critics—and now it's your turn.

Chapter XXIII

In Conclusion

Napoleon Bisson, a dear Canadian colleague of mine, once said, "Becoming an opera singer is like joining a monastery." I do not think that the disciplinary requirements for a career in opera can be better described.

Discipline

There are various kinds of discipline that must be faced, some of which are:

1) A discipline of vocal scales which must be practiced constantly throughout your entire career. Outside of occasional vacations, you should vocalize at least every second day of your life, or even every day if you have a lyric voice. I personally favor a system of scales that runs from twenty to thirty minutes—but which should not be overdone.

2) *A discipline of scales that one should employ a specific number of hours before the curtain goes up*; exactly how many, is up to you. I, personally, like to eat a substantial meal five hours before I step on the stage since it takes my stomach at least four and a half hours to empty. If I perform sooner after a meal than this, I run the risk of being logey from the digestive process. I then vocalize about half an hour after the meal, since eating gives me a momentary lift—and my digestive circulation is not yet sufficiently geared up to interfere with my singing. However, all this is highly personal and you must plan your own schedule.

Carlo Bergonzi told me that he eats his breakfast at 10:00 A.M. and takes nothing else until after the show. But we are all different and each of us must find what suits us best. This is important enough a subject to deserve serious attention.

3) *A discipline of not overdoing your vocal warmup when you are in bad voice.* Under stressful conditions it requires strong discipline on your part to only vocalize at a set time. The worst thing you can do is keep on cudgeling the voice into submission throughout the day. So do your scales and then remain quiet until fifteen or twenty minutes before you go on stage. If you do not heed this advice, you will seriously run the risk of leaving your voice in the dressing room.

4) *A discipline of controlling excessive talking when attending social functions such as public dinners, or when riding in cars or airplanes where there is strong background noise.* Such situations can prove to be quite harmful to the singing voice. It can also be dangerous to talk at length on the telephone. Each of these can be hazardous for the singing voice, but it is most important of all not to talk excessively on the day of a performance, or even the night before.

Many singers not only refuse to go out and visit over lunch or dinner on the day of a show, but even go so far as to avoid social events after a strenuous performance. That, however, is usually not wise. I would advise you to consider it part of the job to participate in any prearranged social event following a performance. It is extremely important to your local sponsor that special donors and volunteers, who have worked so hard behind the scenes, at least have the small reward of meeting with the artists.

5) *A discipline of avoiding any alcoholic beverages on the day of a performance, or even the night before.* Alcohol is notorious for causing edema (redness and swelling) in the mucous tissues, including the vocal folds. In extreme cases, great careers have been lost due to acute alcoholism.

6) *A discipline of remaining single until one's career is well established.* Marriage makes serious demands upon one's time and financial resources, and many a promising career has been aborted because of a premature marriage.

7) *A strong moral discipline, which is especially important for the married singer.* Traveling puts great temptation in the path of the artist who is fortunate enough to be constantly employed on the road. Such a discipline is crucial, since a clear, undisturbed conscience is essential to a successful career.

A colleague of mine, who shall remain nameless, once burst into my dressing room following a performance and slumped over the makeup table, crying out in an anguished voice, "I sang like the worst student today, because my conscience is so filthy..."

Believe me, this is a serious problem. I have seen more than one singer, already deep into a career, face the fact that they cannot resist the temptations that arise when they travel. They were so emotionally torn apart that they eventually abandoned the profession just to save their marriages and their own integrity.

8) *A discipline required to fill the lonely hours.* Consider the stress and boredom associated with spending most of one's life in hotel rooms in strange cities. No one has more spare time than an opera singer on the road. Rehearsals usually require only about two or three hours of the day, so what does one do with all those spare hours when not rehearsing?

This is a tremendous challenge and, for some, a tremendous opportunity. There are those that read extensively and improve their

213

minds. It also affords a great opportunity to do creative work; that is how I have managed to write so many books, music and even operas.

But it is also a time of estrangement from your family, which can be quite trying. Face it, it is not a normal, happy life and requires great adjustment and sacrifice. I am not saying all this to discourage you, but to open your eyes to the realities of the operatic profession. It will take a profound love of singing to be able to make such sacrifices.

What Price a Career?

We have already spoken at length about some of the sacrifices that must be made in order to have an operatic career. Why these sacrifices? If you do not make them, what, exactly, are the dangers that can make or break you?

You cannot believe how many singers I have heard with extraordinary voices who have not made it to the professional stage and never will. Why? Usually because of some particular flaw that could have been corrected if the singer had been willing to accept responsibility for the problem—and had been willing to change.

I am sorry to say this, but I must: if you have an extraordinary voice, and have not made a career, it is quite possibly your own fault. Yes, that is the equivalent of calling you a failure. Now, nobody likes to be called a failure, and people are seldom willing to admit to it, so the commonest escape is to blame something or someone else. I am a firm believer in the saying, "You are not a failure until you blame your failure on someone else."

The trouble is that if you make excuses that constantly relieve you from responsibility for your own shortcomings, you are putting yourself in the position of being a "victim." When you are a "victim," there is nothing you can do to remedy your situation. But, if you accept responsibility for your problem, you are in a position to seek a solution.

At the risk of repeating myself, I will say, When something goes wrong, immediately search for what *you* might have done wrong. In my opinion 95 percent of all my past vocal problems were self-inflicted.

Motivation

What is the core of sustained success in any important endeavor? There will always be great challenges when you struggle to fulfill great dreams, challenges that will surely defeat you should you not fervently believe in your calling and doggedly pursue your goals.

In America's great Civil War, almost all the battles were won by the South, but the North refused to give up. The lesson is clear: It is not how many battles you lose, but Who Wins the War! That is the true core of success: a dogged persistence which will not allow surrender.

When disappointments and defeats confront you, what urges you to fight against seemingly insurmountable odds? What motivation drives you to accomplish what others cannot?

Let us reason together: first, you must honestly assess the real reason why you have chosen the profession of opera. The main attraction should not be the money you hope to make, since so few Americans earn a decent living as opera singers. So if you are ambitious to amass a fortune, think again about choosing opera as your profession: the odds are too poor.

During an interview with Joseph McClellan, critic for the *Washington Post*, he and I got into a discussion on "motivation."

According to McClellan, when some kid says to him, "I want to be a journalist," he comes back with "Kid, you just said the wrong thing. You should have said, 'I love to write.'"

He felt that all these youngsters see is the glamor of their name and picture in print. They are looking for glory, not what really counts. McClellan maintains he never had a pen out of his hand from the age of eleven. He wrote simply because he loved doing it.

I feel this is the core of what should motivate opera singers. It should be a case of "sing or die," not the thrill of being the center of attention on the stage, of being a star! And I must say that this seems to describe the successful opera stars I have known: they love what they are doing with a passion! If you don't feel that way about it, choose another profession.

No matter how much you love to sing there will always be times of intense disappointment, discouragement and even defeat—you cannot win them all. These are the critical times when your motivation must come from deep within you, like a wellspring that never runs dry. Every singer must be relentlessly driven by some sort of inner dynamo that never fails.

I have such a spiritually spawned Grand Old Dynamo without which I would have given up in total hopelessness a quarter of a century ago. What drives you? What keeps you going against all odds?

Why Sing?

A singer is usually constrained to perform music created by someone else, but to a certain extent every vocal performance is a creative act in itself. Honestly confront this creative urge. Is it a case of "Of *me* I sing" or "Of *thee* I sing" or just "Of *what* do I sing?" Really, why do we do it? Join me in examining the philosophy and motivation behind the creative urge found in every art form.

In 1937, I was invited by my former piano teacher, Phoebe James, to come to a reception for her nephew who had just returned from Paris where he had been studying composition. We were to hear some recordings of his latest music, and I was really primed for the occasion, having just cut my first record, which made me a self-styled expert on the subject.

After some refreshments, and a visit to the restroom, I returned to the salon to find the needle was already in the groove for the nephew's first record. I made some wisecrack concerning the all too obvious background noise on the record and, in so doing, really put my foot in it. The "background noise" was actually the "composition"—music made by dropping wooden blocks on the floor. Such was my first encounter with John Cage!

After joining the Met nine years later, I once again faced off with John Cage, this time in my New York apartment where there ensued a two-hour philosophical collision. I was dealt a double dose of artistic gobbledygook about modern music. I had already waded through this modernistic slush before and found it no more attractive, even from a man that had recently become so famous. All I heard that night was, "I write only for myself. I don't care if my music is never heard by anyone else—the important thing is that I express myself. It is not important what my music means to others, it is only important what it meant to me when I wrote it."

John Cage was truly a product of our capricious generation, which is so obsessed with "self-expression." Composers of previous generations always spoke of being inspired by "someone" greater and better than themselves. I cannot help but recall Bruno Walter telling me he believed all great music was the gift of the Holy Spirit of God.

But today's compositions (or decompositions, according to how you look at it), based upon self-expression, are often no more than psychopathology in sound, or simply expression of a self that is not worth expressing.

In today's society, it is hard to be heard without screaming. So, in order to be successful, you must create something that is shockingly different, simply for the sake of being different. The message is secondary, if there is one at all.

Being a mathematician by training, I appreciate the importance of abstraction. But just as in mathematics, any art form, no matter how abstract, should still serve as a means of communication or it will only further contribute to the festering mess we call modern society.

On the lighter side, the night before a concert at a midwestern university, I was invited to the president's home for dinner. When I arrived, he welcomed me warmly and introduced me to his eighteen-year-old daughter. He proudly informed me that she was a freshman at the university and was majoring in art.

217

I was then escorted to a nearby wall where the daughter's first painting had been hung. I silently marvelled that they had hung the painting instead of the artist. Seeing the whimsical look on her father's face, I innocently asked the young artist, "What do you call it? Does it have a title?"

She blithely responded: "Oh, call it whatever you like, Mr. Hines."

"Well, I'm too polite for that," I said, perhaps a bit indiscreetly. "But, ahh...What is it supposed to mean?"

"Whatever it means to you," she said, smiling patronizingly.

Shades of Cage; I had already had my fill of that over the years, but I struggled to be more polite.

"What did it mean to you when you painted it?" I asked.

She shrugged and said, "Nothing, really!"

"Then why did you paint it?" She seemed a bit confused by the question, and then giggled, saying, "Just to get your attention, I guess."

"Well, now that you have my attention, what do you have to say?" I asked.

Obviously empathizing with me, her father burst out laughing, and mother saved the day by announcing that dinner was served.

So this is the crazy world we live in, and the question is "How is the singer to fit creatively into all this?"

Well, let the singer honestly ask, "Why am I doing this? Why do I sing?"

I believe the answer should simply be, "Because it is a joy to sing and I want to share my joy with others." So let us daily serve great Art and our fellow man—*not* ourselves.

Should I, or Should I Not?

There will be times when you will be called upon to do things on the stage which you will personally consider offensive, and the question is "What should you do?" You are not alone in this sort of dilemma: it happens occasionally to all of us and the decision you make can possibly affect your future in the profession.

In 1967, the Metropolitan Opera staged a new production of *Faust* and I was contracted to sing the role of Mephistopheles in four performances at the house and four on the tour. I was in the second cast and when I attended the dress rehearsal I was shocked to see that the Walpurgis scene had been turned into a sordid display of pornography.

I went to Rudolf Bing's office the next day and told him there was no way I was going to set foot on the stage in that scene the way it was staged. He tried to convince me that the filthier the Walpurgis scene's staging, the more powerful the Christian finale would be. Furthermore, he tried to convince me that what I did on the stage had nothing to do with what I believed in real life. His arguments did not move me and I stood fast on my refusal to take part in such a scene.

Bob Herman, Mr. Bing's Assistant Manager, suggested that when I performed, they could delete the scene, a suggestion Mr. Bing rejected out of hand. He then stormed out of the office shouting that he felt all this was "just a cheap attempt on my part to get some free publicity."

Since I was breaking my contract by refusing to sing in Bing's new *Faust* production, this could have terminated my Met career. Two days later Mr. Bing notified me by letter that I had been replaced in *Faust* and that he still thought I was being very childish to refuse to do the production.

I must add that the critics found the staging to be shamelessly and unnecessarily pornographic. The public booed the show so loudly in subsequent performances that Mr. Bing had to place security guards in the hall to eject unruly members of the audience.

I, personally, paid quite a price. Mephistopheles in *Faust* has been one of the two most important roles in my career and was the first major part I played at the Met. I was never to perform it there again! Frankly, I prefer to have paid such a price and not have compromised my integrity.

We all remember Nedda Casei as a fine artist and as the president of AGMA, the American Guild of Musical Artists. She was cast in a

Met production of *Mahagonny*. During the show's preparation, John Dexter, the stage director required her to make an obscene gesture and she refused to do it. He told her that if she did not relent over the weekend, he would take her out of the cast. Many of the company, including choristers, rallied behind her and it became a hot issue. The following week, Dexter backed down and assigned the action to another person. Nedda was off the hook and we were all relieved—and very proud of her.

There are provisions made by AGMA which give you the right to refuse to do certain things on the stage which you find offensive. How much real support the union can and will give you is questionable. But keep it in mind.

Is It Fair?

Should you expect to be treated fairly in the opera business? Some very fine and honorable artists seem rather skeptical, or even cynical, about fairness in the profession.

But, certainly, not everyone on the other side of the fence in the opera business is a scoundrel. We singers must consider the special problems faced by the impresario and the opera manager. They, too, are under great stress, and it is an entirely different kind of stress from that suffered by the singer—but stress it is.

Impresarios often have to make hard decisions involving choices between two artists, decisions which will clearly profit one and cause the other to suffer. How does an impresario explain a particular choice to the offended artist? Not all people possess the toughness of character to tell the truth in touchy situations. In fact, there are even some people who simply have no concern for the truth.

Do not be surprised if and when you are treated unfairly. Let me give you a typical example of the sort of thing that can happen, and did happen to "yours truly" in the early fifties.

It was a general rule at the Met that the second cast for a production was never given a stage rehearsal. In the Met's 1951/52 season, I was performing the role of Pimen in *Boris Godunov* with

George London in the title role. When Cesare Siepi was about to take over the title role in the second cast, we were all called to do a full rehearsal on the main stage. Since that was unheard of, I asked Max Rudolph why the precedent was being broken. His response was, "You cannot expect an artist to do the first Boris of his life without a rehearsal on the stage."

During the following Met season, when I was to do the first Boris of *my* life, I very pointedly asked Max Rudolph when I was going to have my rehearsal on the main stage. The answer was, "Surely, an artist of your stature doesn't need a stage rehearsal."

Did he mean that I was an artist of greater stature than Cesare Siepi? Of course not! It was simply a shallow dodge to avoid the fact that there was a double standard in the way American artists and foreign artists were treated.

Believe me, I was not the only one who felt the sting of that discrimination. A classic example of how great American artists of my generation felt about that double standard was most evident in the Met's performance of *La Forza del Destino* the night Leonard Warren died on the stage. (Despite Rudolf Bing's erroneous claim in *Twenty Thousand Nights at the Opera* that Cesare Siepi was the Guardiano in that fateful performance, I was actually the one who sang the role—so do not believe everything you read.) Here is what happened backstage that night.

The occasion was the return of Renata Tebaldi after a two year absence. When she appeared in the opening scene, there was a four minute ovation before she sang her first note. That came as no surprise to me since I was a real Tebaldi fan. But, during that ovation, Leonard Warren walked into my dressing room and said sarcastically, "What are we doing here? Why should we waste our time? Since we are only Americans, we might as well go home."

As he turned to leave my dressing room, Richard Tucker flung the door open with, "Hey kid, what are we doing here? Who needs us? Just because we are Americans..." And the same bitter complaint ensued.

221

These two American superstars were deeply disturbed and, believe me, they went on the stage thirsting for blood. Now Leonard had always been a rather laid back singer, but those who were out front that night said it was the first time they had ever heard him give his all—which he apparently did—and dropped dead on the stage after heroically delivering his big aria.

American artists of my generation never felt they were being treated fairly by either the management or the public. However, with the advent of James Levine at the Met, the American artists have recently come into their own. Without question, unfairness can take on many other forms, so do not be surprised when it shows up in your life.

The Trinity of Truth

The Book of Proverbs constantly refers to Knowledge, Understanding and Wisdom, which I like to call "The Trinity of Truth."

"Knowledge" is related to the past, being data you have stored in your mind over the years gone by.

"Understanding" is related to the present, being your capacity as of now to relate the data and act upon it.

"Wisdom" relates to the future and comes into play when you must make a decision for future action and do not have all the facts and understanding to make the best course of action clear.

"Wisdom" is the hardest to deal with, since it either involves some sort of Divine guidance or the frustrating alternatives of simply rolling the dice or flipping a coin. You probably have heard enough about me to know which Way I have taken, so I will not bother you any further on that.

Now, I am not sure whether I should say, "God bless you" or just wish you "Good luck." Whatever path you choose for yourself is your business, so choose well, my friend, since your life and career will depend upon it. Either way, I do wish you well.

JERRY HINES

222

APPENDIX I

Back in the early sixties the United States Navy conducted extensive experiments in an attempt to communicate with dolphins. Now, dolphins are known to be quite intelligent and appear to have a highly complex language. The USN personnel hoped to be able to train them to carry out underwater military missions and an attempt was made to understand their language. But, there was one big problem: the sounds by which dolphins communicate have frequencies as high as 200,000 vibrations per second, whereas the human ear cannot handle frequencies as high as a mere 12,000. To further complicate the issue, language is based, not so much on pitch, as on vowels and consonants. One key question was, what is a vowel at, say, over 100,000 vibrations per second? It became critical to be able to define more clearly what a vowel really is. Here is how it was resolved: a vowel is the ear's and brain's perception of "phase difference." What, then, is "phase difference"?

Sound waves are carried by some medium such as air or water. If there is no medium to carry the sound waves, there is simply no sound. For example, in the empty vacuum of outer space, there is no medium to carry sound waves, so astronauts must communicate by means other than sound, unless they are able to physically touch their space helmets together, which is not always practical.

When a transmitting source emits sound waves of a certain pitch, they are all of the same exact frequency. For example, when a tuning-fork sounds what we call "the standard A," the pitch at which most symphony and operatic orchestras are tuned, all of the sound waves emitted by the tuning-fork have exactly the same frequency of 440 vibrations per second.

Sound waves can be made to issue from a transmitter so that all of them are "in phase," which simply means that they are "waving in unison." In other words, as two of those waves travel parallel to each other and troughs are in perfect alignment, as in Diagram I.1:

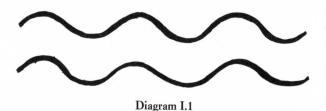

Diagram I.1

These waves are said to be "in phase." Two waves, with their crests and troughs out of alignment, as in Diagram I.2:

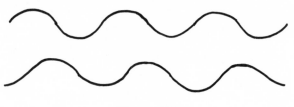

Diagram I.2

are said to be "out of phase."

Now, if the "in phase" waves of Diagram I.1 are bounced off a reflecting surface, as pictured in Diagram I.3:

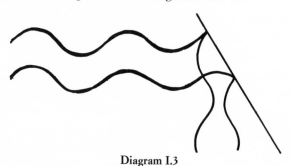

Diagram I.3

the lower wave hits the reflecting surface after the upperwave does, knocking the two waves "out of phase." Their crests and troughs are no longer lined up together, and the amount that they are "out of phase" is called the "phase difference." Of course, the "phase difference" varies according to the angle of the reflecting surface, and it is this "phase difference" that the ear registers and the brain interprets as "vowel" sound.

This means that we can go from one vowel to another, simply by bouncing the waves off a reflecting surface at some particular angle. Independent of the transmitting source, the vowel becomes a product of the angle at which it is reflected. This applies to the human voice in an interesting way. It means that we should be able to go from one vowel to another with absolutely no change in the transmitter (namely the vocal folds), merely by altering the positions of the jaw and tongue.

The very obvious fact that many immature singers tend to favor one type of vowel over another on high notes, demonstrates that they are manipulating the transmitter (the larynx) from vowel to vowel. All vowels should be equally easy in all parts of one's range.

APPENDIX II

The following is a chart that clearly delineates the differences in terminology used by male and female singers:

	MALE	FEMALE
1st Voice	Chest Voice	Belting (Raw Chest)
2nd Voice	Middle Voice	Chest Voice
3rd Voice	High Voice	Middle Voice
4th Voice	Falsetto	High Voice